ISBN 978-0-483-71233-1
PIBN 10849237

"The words that I speak unto you, they are spirit, and they are life."—JESUS

SPIRIT AND LIFE

A COLLECTION OF SONGS FOR THE

Sunday School, Young People's Societies Devotional Meetings, and Revival Services

PREPARED BY

REV. E. S. LORENZ AND REV. D. E. DORTCH

ASSISTED BY

REV W. T. DALE AND JAMES H. RUEBUSH

DAYTON, OHIO
LORENZ & CO., MUSIC PUBLISHERS
1895

PREFACE.

"SPIRIT AND LIFE." Perhaps a presumptuous title, but the authors feel that this collection of songs will bring enthusiasm and vigor into any Sunday-school or church service where it may be used, so that in the ordinary sense of the words the title is not an inappropriate one. We trust, however, that our songs will also bring the deeper, truer blessing of the spirit and life that abide in the words of Christ, and that even in this spiritual sense the title of the book is not a misnomer. The many singers represented in this book come from the North and South, the East and West; some of them have been singing for years, others have tried their wings for the first time; some incline to one type of doctrine and church life, and some to another: but they all sing the same "song of Moses and the Lamb." We have made an earnest endeavor to serve the churches of the land with a symmetrical, practical, stirring, and helpful collection of songs. We trust that out of this rich provision of new songs a few will be found worthy to live after the writers have passed into the land where they shall sing forever.

SPIRIT AND LIFE.

1. SING HALLELUJAH.

MARK ADAMS. JOHN TIBBALLS.

1. I wander'd once in woe and shame, My life was lost in sin's fierce flame;
2. I wander'd far, but found no peace, From sin's a-larms no glad release;
3. I once was weak and passion's slave, And Satan's on - set dared not brave;
4. A son of God, a child of light, With hope and joy my life is bright;
Now I be-lieve in Je-sus' name, My soul is sav'd, sing hal-le - lu - jah!
But Je-sus bade my struggles cease, And I am sav'd, sing hal-le - lu - jah!
But Christ has pow'r the weak to save, And I am sav'd, sing hal-le - lu - jah!
De-spair and gloom have taken flight, For I am sav'd, sing hal-le - lu - jah!
CHORUS.
Sing hal - le - lu - jah, I am sav'd! Sing hal - le - lu - jah, I am sav'd!
From sin and shame, thro' Jesus' name, My soul is sav'd, sing hal-le - lu - jah!

2. THE SPIRIT OF CHRIST.

W. R. WILLIAM RUSSELL.

1. The spir - it of Christ is love, true love, That flow- eth a - bound-ing and free; 'Tis of- fered to ev - 'ry faint - ing soul, 'Tis of- fered to you and me.
2. The spir - it of Christ is joy, pure joy, Un- speak - a - ble, glo - ri - ous, bright; It lifts up the soul that's bend - ing low, And leads us in - to the light.
3. The spir - it of Christ is peace, sweet peace, That qui - ets the tem-pest-tossed soul; In trou- ble it gives us sweet re - lief, It com-forts and makes us whole.
CHORUS.
If a - ny man have not the spir - it of Christ He is none of His, none of His; If an - y man have not the spir - it of Christ He is none of His, none of His.

Controlled by D. E. Dortch.

3. WELCOME THE SPIRIT IN.

ANNA CHICHESTER. E. S. LORENZ.

1. O - pen your heart to - the Spir-it's en-treat-ing, Welcome him in!
2. Life all di - vine doth the Spir - it now prof-fer; Welcome him in!
3. Fruits more than gold-en this Spir - it will yield you; Welcome him in!
4. He is a friend that a - bid-eth for - ev - er; Welcome him in!
welcome him in! List to his wings at your heart's windows beat-ing,
welcome him in! Life that's e - ter - nal—ac - cept now his of - fer,
welcome him in! Love, peace, and joy, when his grace shall have seal'd you,
welcome him in! He brings a com - fort that fail - eth you nev - er;
Wel-come the Spir - it in!
CHORUS.
Wel-come him in, he has blessing un-told; Welcome him in, peace your heart shall en - fold;
Welcome him in, love your spirit shall hold, Welcome the Spir-it in!

4. THE FIELD OF THE MASTER.

JENNIE CRANSTON. W. A. OGDEN.

1. To the field of the Mas-ter let us has - ten a - way; And the
2. To the field of the Mas-ter we will go with his word; There are
3. In the field of the Mas-ter hear the shout and the song; 'Tis the
grain ripe for har-vest we'll gar - ner to - day; In the strength of the
sheaves to be gath-ered and grain to be stored; We will has - ten to
voice of the reap - ers now march-ing a - long, Sing-ing "Glo - ry to
Mas-ter we our courage renew, And we'll do with our might what our hands find to do.
gar-ner it, or some may be lost; For the season is passing, soon cometh the frost.
Jesus, who hath died on the tree, And forever a ran-som for sin-ners is he."
REFRAIN.
Striv - ing on, ... striv - ing on, ... For-ward
striv - ing on, striv - ing on,
go, ... for-ward go, ... With his pres-ence to cheer us, we will
Forward go, forward go,

THE FIELD OF THE MASTER. Concluded.

work with a will, And we'll strive with our might all our task to ful-fill.

5. THE LOVE OF JESUS.

CAPT. C. MERRITT. E. HANKS.

1. Bright-ly beams thy love, Lord Je - sus, Sweet the peace that fills my soul;
2. Once I walked in sin and dark-ness, Stumbled oft and deep-ly fell;
3. Now I strive each day to serve him, Tell-ing friends who know him not
4. Make me, Christ, a loy - al sol - dier, Ev - er read - y at my post,
FINE.
Joy e - ter - nal, love so bound-less, Keep me while the a - ges roll.
But he called, and when I an-swered, Light he gave and all was well.
How the dear Christ has re-deemed me, How for them he long has sought.
Nev - er shirk-ing a - ny du - ty, Seek-ing those who need thee most.
D.S.—Ev - er in the path of du - ty, seek - ing pre-cious souls to save.
CHORUS.
D. S.
Sat - is - fy my heart's deep yearning, Keep me, Je - sus, true and brave;

6. WHY NOT BE SAVED?

ANNA CHICHESTER. FRED. W. GILBERT.

1. Oh, why do you wait, Why long - er de - bate, When the Sav- iour in love is call - ing? He know- eth your needs And ten - der - ly pleads; Shall his words on deaf ears be fall - ing?
2. Shall ten - der- ness fail, O'er you not pre - vail, And shall love beg in vain for hear - ing? Shall mer - cy soon cease Its of - fers of peace, Leav-ing you to the doom that's near - ing?
3. With Christ in your heart A new life will start, Whose de - light will be e'er in - creas - ing; For trou - ble and care, For sor - row, de- spair, You will gain a deep peace un - ceas - ing.
4. Oh, why will you die, When Christ is so nigh With his of - fers of love en - treat - ing? Oh, yield to him now, Sub- mis - sive - ly bow, On your heart's throne the Sav- iour seat - ing.
CHORUS.
Why not be saved to-night?* Why not be saved to-night?
Why not be sav'd to - night?* Why not be sav'd to - night?
Je- sus is call - ing; lin-ger no more, En- ter love's o - pen door.

* To be sung "to-night" or "to-day," according to the hour of service.

7. SAVED BY FAITH.

I. B. REV. IS. BALTZELL.

1. I have found redemption in the Saviour's blood, I am sav'd by faith in his blood, in his blood; I am sweetly trust-ing in the word of God, I am sav'd by faith in his blood.
2. Oh, how sweet the story of his wondrous grace, I am sav'd by faith in his blood, in his blood; I will trust in Je-sus while I run my race, I am
3. I will sing of Je-sus while the days go by, I am sav'd by faith in his blood, in his blood; I will trust his promise, on his strength re-ly, I am
4. I will keep on sing-ing as I march a-long, I am sav'd by faith in his blood, in his blood; In my home in glo-ry this shall be my song, I am
CHORUS.
I am saved, . . . yes, sweetly sav'd,
I am sav'd, sweetly sav'd, I am sav'd, sweetly sav'd,
1
I am sav'd by faith in the blood he shed for me,
2
I am sav'd by faith in his blood,
in his blood.

By permission.

8. THE FRUITS OF THE SPIRIT.

W. L. BENNETT. CHAS. EDW. POLLOCK.

1. There's a love that's be-got - ten with - in, When the work of re -
2. There's a joy of un-speak - a - ble worth, That's more glo-rious than
3. There a peace like a riv - er doth flow, Pure and free from the
4. May our hearts with this love o - ver - flow, Un - to us may this
demp - tion is done; When the soul is de - liv - ered from
tongue can de - clare; Je - sus brought this rich bless - ing to
bright realms of day; God this won - der - ful gift will be -
pure joy be given; May this peace be our por - tion be -
sin, Through the blood of the cru - ci - fied One.
earth, That the world heav'n's re - joic - ing might share.
stow, Up - on all who his pre - cepts o - bey.
low, Our re - ward in the king - dom of heav'n.
CHORUS.
In the sweet by and by, 1. We shall
2. We shall
3. We shall
In the sweet by and by, 4. In the

dwell in the full - ness of love, In our blest . . . . .
dwell in the full - ness of joy, In our blest . . . . .
dwell in the full - ness of peace, In our blest . . . . .
full - ness of joy, peace and love, May we all . . . . .
by and by,
home on high, ... In the beau - ti - ful mansions a - bove.
home on high, ... Where glad songs the long a - ges em - ploy.
home on high, ... Where the wick - ed from troubling shall cease.
meet on high, ... In the beau - ti - ful man-sions a - bove.

9. PRAISE THE LORD.

JOHN KEMPTHORN. WEBER.

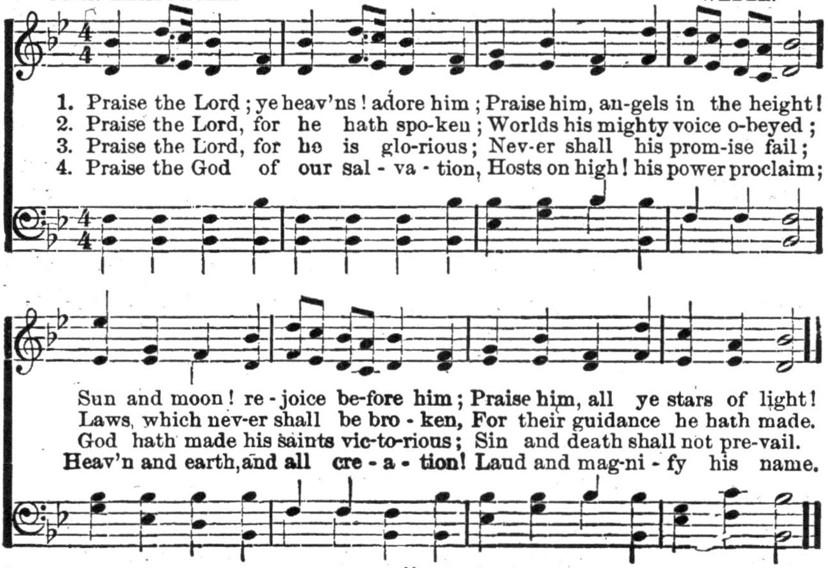
1. Praise the Lord; ye heav'ns! adore him; Praise him, an-gels in the height!
2. Praise the Lord, for he hath spo-ken; Worlds his mighty voice o-beyed;
3. Praise the Lord, for he is glo-rious; Nev-er shall his prom-ise fail;
4. Praise the God of our sal - va - tion, Hosts on high! his power proclaim;
Sun and moon! re - joice be-fore him; Praise him, all ye stars of light!
Laws, which nev-er shall be bro - ken, For their guidance he hath made.
God hath made his saints vic-to-rious; Sin and death shall not pre-vail.
Heav'n and earth, and all cre - a - tion! Laud and mag-ni - fy his name.

10. SOWING IN TEARS.

EDEN R. LATTA. E. S. LORENZ.

DUET.
1. Sow - ing in tears, sor - row-ful tears, Oft - en the faith - ful go, Go with the seed, spir - it - ual seed, That Je-sus bids them sow!
2. Sow - ing in tears, sor - row-ful tears, Jour-ney - ing to and fro, Bear - ing the seed, spir - it - ual seed, Sav - ing from end-less woe!
3. Sow - ing in tears, sor - row-ful tears, Tar - ry - ing here be - low, Bear - ing the seed, glo - ri - ous seed, That Je-sus bids them strew!
Reap - ing in joy, Grain from their la - bor
Reap - ing in joy, Souls that are saved from
Reap - ing in joy, Sheaves that had nev - er
Reap-ing in joy, rap-tur-ous joy,
Reap-ing in joy, rap-tur-ous joy,
Reap-ing in joy, heav-en-ly joy,

SOWING IN TEARS. Concluded.

grown! Grown from the seed, They in their tears had sown.
sin! Souls that were lost, Strove in their tears to win!
grown, But for the seed, Seed in their weeping sown!
Grown from the seed, glorious seed,
Souls that were lost, souls that they strove,
But for the seed, soul-saving seed,
CHORUS.
Sow-ing in tears, sor-row-ful tears! Hard is their lot, but oh!
Bet-ter it is, bet-ter it is, Bet-ter than not to sow.

11. SENTENCE.

W. F. McCAULEY.

Not that we loved God, but that he loved us and { sent his Son to / be the propiti- } a-tion for our sins.

12. THE GOOD SAMARITAN.

W. M. R. REV. W. M. ROBISON.

1. From Je - ru - sa - lem to Jer - i - cho, a thoughtless youth did go,
2. From Je - ru - sa - lem to Jer - i - cho, a priest and Le - vite went,
3. From Je - ru - sa - lem to Jer - i - cho, in coars - er gar - ment clad,
4. From Je - ru - sa - lem to Jer - i - cho, we're trav-'ling ev - 'ry day,
Think-ing on - ly of him-self and on the things of earth be-low;
Think-ing on - ly of themselves and, on some sel- fish mis - sion bent;
There came a good Sa-mar - i - tan, who great compas - sion had;
And ma - ny are the dy - ing ones who lie a-long the way;
He fell a-mong the thieves who beat him, leav-ing him to die,
They saw the wound-ed trav - el - er and heard his bro - ken cry,
He went un - to the trav - el - er, he gave him of his store,
Are you a good Sa-mar - i - tan with love as warm and wide,
D.S.—From Je - ru - sa - lem to Jer - i - cho we're traveling ev - 'ry day,
FINE.
And none were near to of - fer aid, or hear his fee - ble cry.
And tho' they each did pit - y him, with pride they pass'd him by.
And from his scan - ty purse we see him still pro- vid - ing more.
Or do you like those priestly ones pass by on th' oth - er side?
And ma - ny are the dy - ing ones who lie a - long the way.

THE GOOD SAMARITAN. Concluded.

CHORUS.
Then who, tell me who, Tell me
tell me who, then who, tell me who,
who was his neigh-bor kind and true,
kind and true?
D. S.

13. HOLY SPIRIT, FAITHFUL GUIDE.

M. M. W. M. M. WELLS.

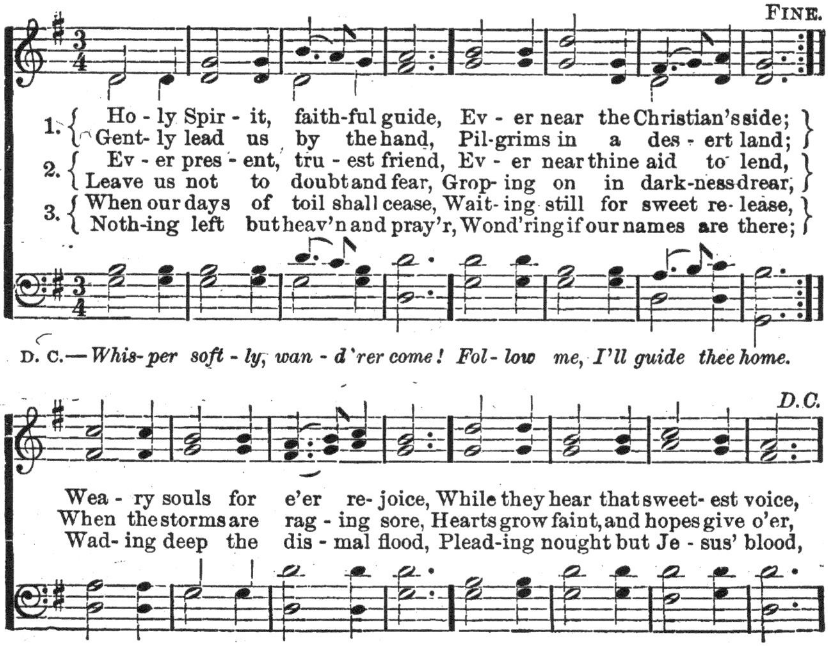
FINE.
1. { Ho - ly Spir - it, faith-ful guide, Ev - er near the Christian's side;
Gent- ly lead us by the hand, Pil-grims in a des - ert land; }
2. { Ev - er pres - ent, tru - est friend, Ev - er near thine aid to lend,
Leave us not to doubt and fear, Grop- ing on in dark-ness drear; }
3. { When our days of toil shall cease, Wait- ing still for sweet re- lease,
Noth-ing left but heav'n and pray'r, Wond'ring if our names are there; }
D. C.—Whis-per soft - ly, wan - d'rer come! Fol- low me, I'll guide thee home.
D.C.
Wea - ry souls for e'er re- joice, While they hear that sweet- est voice,
When the storms are rag - ing sore, Hearts grow faint, and hopes give o'er,
Wad- ing deep the dis - mal flood, Plead-ing nought but Je - sus' blood,

14. CALL THEM IN.

ANNA CHICHESTER. E. S. LORENZ.

1. Call them in, hear the King in love command-ing, Call the wand'rers who
2. Call them in, for their hearts are torn and bleed-ing, And they long for the
3. Call them in, spread the roy - al in - vi - ta - tion, Tell the love that the
4. Call them in! O the joy of earn - est call-ing! Joy the an - gels on
'mid the hedg-es lie; While in sloth and in i - dle-ness we're standing,
sym - pa - thy di-vine; Then with joy to their help let us be speeding,
feast for them prepared; All ye ser-vants of God, whate'er your sta-tion,
high de - light to share; When they come from the doom of death ap-pall - ing,
Shall their souls in the dark-ness pine and die?
On their hearts cause the light of life to shine.
Call them in, for the King for them has cared.
In your heart springs a joy be - yond compare.
CHORUS.
Call them in!
Call them in!
the King has sent you!
call them in! let naught pre-
the King has sent you! call them in! Call them in! . . . . . let naught pre-
vent you!
vent you! call them in! Call them in! for your work will ne'er re -

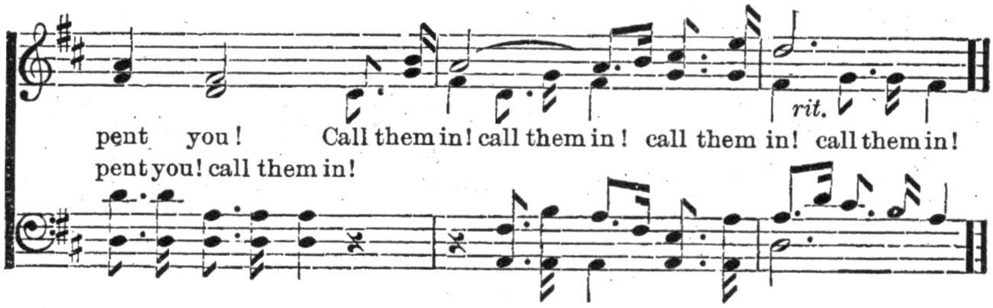
rit.
pent you! Call them in! call them in! call them in! call them in!
pent you! call them in!

15. PASS UNDER THE ROD.

REV. W. T. DALE. D. E. DORTCH.

1. When bow'd with af-flic-tions and woes here be-low, As on in my way to bright Canaan I go, I hear a sweet voice—'tis the voice of my God:
2. 'Mid tri-als and loss-es, 'mid sorrows and fears, When mingling the cup of thanksgiving and tears, I hear the same voice, the sweet voice of my God:
3. When weeping I stand o'er the spoils of the grave, My friends all de-part-ed be-yond the dark wave, I hear the soft voice of my Fa-ther and God:
"I love thee, I love thee, pass un-der the rod."
REFRAIN.
Pass un-der the rod, pass under the rod,
rit.
I love thee, I love thee; pass un-der the rod.

16. THE SPIRIT OF GOD.

E. H. E. HANKS.

1. Is the spir - it of God lead- ing you, broth-er, Does his
2. Is the spir - it of God lead- ing you, broth-er, Do you
3. Is the spir - it of God lead-ing you, broth-er, Do you
com-fort, joy and peace o'er you roll? Are you wash'd in the blood of the
fol - low at his call ev - 'ry day? Are you faith-ful - ly walk- ing with
lis - ten for his voice in your breast? Are your feet on the Rock, firm and
Lamb, broth-er, Do you feel its cleans-ing pow'r in your soul?
him, broth-er, Are you ea - ger his com-mands to o - bey?
strong, broth-er, Do you long to reach that sweet heav - 'nly rest?
CHORUS.
As ma- ny as are led by the spir - it of God, By the
spir- it of God, by the spir - it of God, As ma- ny as are

THE SPIRIT OF GOD. Concluded.

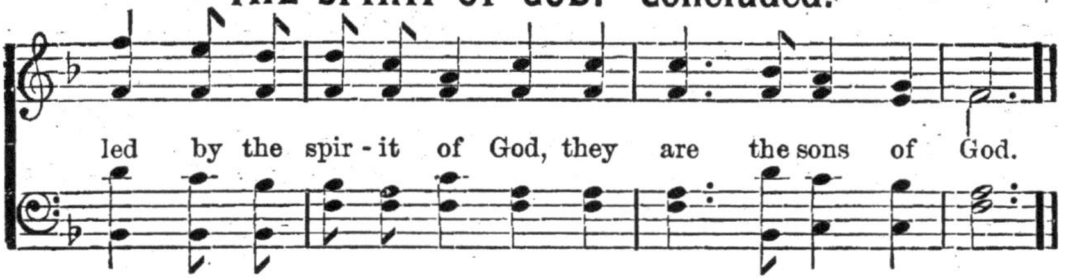
led by the spir - it of God, they are the sons of God.

17. GOD'S FLOWERS.

Dedicated to the King's Daughters of America.

WILLIAM H. GARDNER. EDWIN MOORE.

1. Gath- er flow - ers from the mead-ow, Car- ry them to sick and lame,
2. One sweet bunch of mead-ow vio- lets, Laid up-on a pil-low white,
3. Some poor heart will dream of childhood, And the dear old gar - den there;
4. Live your life a - lone for oth - ers, Work for Christ of Cal - va - ry!
For it is the flow- ers' mis- sion, To bring sunshine back a- gain.
Brings the light to eyes most fad - ed, Thrills the sad heart with delight.
And you then can soft - ly tell them, Of the "oth - er man-sions fair."
Gath-er flow - ers for the sick-room, Aid in na-ture's min - is- try.
God the flowers gave un- to us, To re -mind us all of heav'n,
So be sure that to earth's suf-f'rers, Glimpses of a- bove are giv'n.

18. SUNSHINE IN THE SOUL.

E. E. HEWITT. JNO. R. SWENEY.

1. There's sun-shine in my soul to-day, More glo-ri-ous and bright
2. There's mu-sic in my soul to-day, A car-ol to my King;
3. There's springtime in my soul to-day, For when the Lord is near,
4. There's glad-ness in my soul to-day, And hope, and praise, and love,
Than glows in an-y earth-ly sky, For Je-sus is my light.
And Je-sus, list-en-ing, can hear The songs I can-not sing.
The dove of peace sings in my heart, The flowers of grace ap-pear.
For bless-ings which he gives me now, For joys "laid up" a-bove.
REFRAIN.
Oh, there's sun - - - - - - shine, Bless-ed sun - - - - - - shine,
sun-shine in the soul, sun-shine in the soul,
While the peace-ful, hap-py mo-ments roll; When
hap-py mo-ments roll,
Je-sus shows his smil-ing face There is sun-shine in the soul.

19. PRAISE HIM EVER.

H. F. JAMES. E. S. LORENZ.

1. Songs of a - dor - a-tion raise, Bring the Lord ex- alt-ed praise, Fill his
2. Praise the Lord with heart and voice, Let his children aye rejoice, As they
3. He who saved us from our sin, Made us whole and pure within, Is a
4. Walking with us all the way, Fill-ing night with heaven's day, All our
courts with glad ac-claim; Grate-ful hearts a-dor - ing bend, Prais-ing
count his mer - cies o'er. Prais-ing him is heavenly joy, Souls re -
friend all friends a - bove; He has called us sons and heirs, Borne our
foes he doth de - feat. Grateful hearts, with gladness thrill, With his
love that knows no end; Lift the voice, ex - alt his name.
deemed their powers em-ploy, Greet with praise the heaven-ly shore.
sor - rows and our cares, Poured on us his wealth of love.
praise the wide earth fill, All his grace and love re - peat.
CHORUS.
Praise him ev-er, all ye sons of men, him, the crucified, him, who for us died;
Tell the sto - ry of his love a - gain, Love de-serv-ing all our praise.

20. BLESSED BE THE NAME.

W. H. CLARK. C. M. Arr. by WM. J. KIRKPATRICK.

1. All praise to him who reigns a - bove; In maj - es - ty su - preme;
2. His name a - bove all names shall stand, Ex - alt - ed more and more,
3. Re - deem - er, Sav-iour, Friend of man, Once ru - in'd by the fall,
4. His name shall be the Coun-sel - lor, The might-y Prince of Peace,
Who gave his Son for man to die, That he might man re-deem.
At God the Fa-ther's own right hand, Where an-gel hosts a - dore.
Thou hast de - vised sal - va-tion's plan, For thou hast died for all.
Of all earth's kingdoms Con-quer-or, Whose reign shall nev-er cease.
CHORUS.
Bless - ed be the name, bless - ed be the name,
Bless - ed be the name of the Lord; Bless - ed be the name,
bless - ed be the name, Bless - ed be the name of the Lord.

By permission.

21. THE COMING OF THE LORD DRAWETH NIGH.

REV. J. H. MARTIN. D. E. DORTCH.

1. Ye peo-ple of the Lord bowed with grief, Who weep and mourn and long
2. In sor-row are you bear-ing the cross, Af - flict-ed, tried, as gold
3. When sins and fears and doubts vex thy soul, When trials fierce like waves
4. Press on, press on with zeal in the race; Thy God will give thee strength
for re - lief, Lift up your heads; be glad; cease to sigh, The
purged of dross; With joy endure, your hope fix on high, The
o'er thee roll, Have faith, for all will end by and by, The
give thee grace; Faint not, but hear a voice from the sky, The
coming of the Lord draw-eth nigh.
coming of the Lord draw-eth nigh.
coming of the Lord draw-eth nigh.
coming of the Lord draw-eth nigh.
CHORUS.
Re - joice in hope, for the
Lord will come; Rejoice in hope, for the Lord will come; Rejoice in hope,
for the Lord will come, And take you up to a bliss - ful home.

22. I AM THE WAY.

C. H. G. CHAS. H. GABRIEL.

1. In from the highways, In from the by- ways, Gather souls in Je-sus'
2. Go to the err - ing, Kind-ly and cheer-ing, Point them to the Cru-ci -
3. Go, then, believ- ing, Bless-ing re-ceiv - ing, You shall reap re - ward a -
name; Publish the sto - ry, Her-ald his glo - ry, Un- to the world his
fied; Res-cue the pray'rless, Plead with the careless, Till they in Je - sus
bove; Je-sus is call - ing,—Darkness is fall-ing, On with the bless-ed
message pro - claim.
safe - ly a - bide.
lab - or of love.
CHORUS.
I am the Way, the Truth, I am the
I am the Way, the Truth, the Life, I am the
Life, ... Come without mon - ey, free - ly will I
Way, the Truth, the Life, Come without mon-ey free - ly,
give; . . . . . I am the Way, the Truth, I am the
free - ly will I give; I am the Way, the Truth, the Life, I am the

Copyright, 1890, by Chas. H. Gabriel. Used by permission.

Life, ... Come unto me, Oh, come and ye shall live. . . . .
Way, the Truth, the Life, Come unto me, Oh, come to me, and ye shall live.

23. DRINK AND LIVE.

IDA L. REED. FRANK M. DAVIS.

1. Come, drink of life's crys- tal fount - ain, Drink, drink and live;
2. Come, drink of life's crys- tal fount - ain, Leave thy sad soul
3. Come, drink of life's crys- tal fount - ain, Thirst - y or sad;
The draught to thee life e - ter - nal Sure - ly will give.
Deep down where its shin- ing bil - lows Cease - less - ly roll.
'Twill be to thee life e - ter - nal, Drink and be glad.
CHORUS.
Come, drink of life's fount - ain, Drink, drink and
Come, drink of life's crys - tal fount - ain,
live, Come, thirst-y, wea- ry, and way-worn, Drink, drink and live.
and live,

24. WAITING AT THE PORTAL.

K. M. REASONER. T. C. O'KANE.

1. I am wait-ing for the Mas-ter, Who will rise and bid me come
2. Many a wea - ry path I've travelled In the dark-est storm and strife,
3. Ma - ny friends who traveled with me Reach'd that portal long a - go,
4. Yes, their pil - grim-age was short-er, And their triumph soon-er won;
To the glo - ry of his presence, To the glad-ness of his home.
Bear - ing many a heav - y bur-den, Oft-en struggling for my life.
One by one have left me bat-tling With the dark and craft - y foe.
Oh how lov - ing - ly they'll greet me When the toils of life are done!
CHORUS.
They are watch - - ing at the por - tal, They are
watch-ing, they are wait-ing,
wait - - ing at the door; Waiting on - - ly for my
waiting, they are watching, on-ly, wait-ing on-ly
com-ing, All the loved . . . . ones gone be - fore.
loved ones, all the loved

By permission.

25. QUICKLY COME.

LORELLE DAMON. D. E. DORTCH.

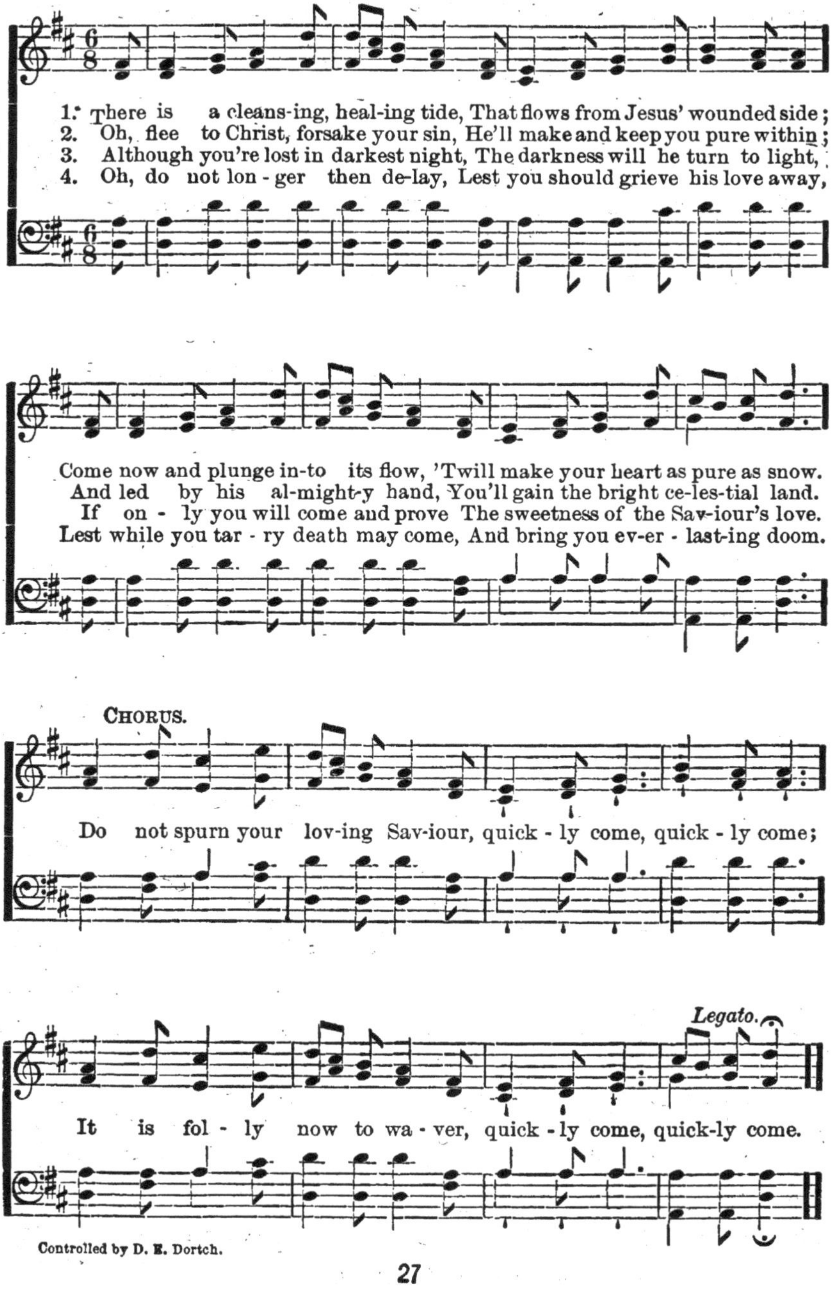
1. There is a cleans-ing, heal-ing tide, That flows from Jesus' wounded side;
2. Oh, flee to Christ, forsake your sin, He'll make and keep you pure within;
3. Although you're lost in darkest night, The darkness will he turn to light,
4. Oh, do not lon - ger then de-lay, Lest you should grieve his love away,
Come now and plunge in-to its flow, 'Twill make your heart as pure as snow.
And led by his al-might-y hand, You'll gain the bright ce-les-tial land.
If on - ly you will come and prove The sweetness of the Sav-iour's love.
Lest while you tar - ry death may come, And bring you ev-er - last-ing doom.
CHORUS.
Do not spurn your lov-ing Sav-iour, quick - ly come, quick - ly come;
Legato.
It is fol - ly now to wa - ver, quick - ly come, quick-ly come.

Controlled by D. E. Dortch.

26. WHEN WE ALL GET HOME OVER THERE.

D. E. D. — D. E. DORTCH.

1. There are man-sions for the blest, Where we ev - er - more shall rest,
2. In that ci - ty of pure gold, Sweet-est pleas-ures will un - fold,
3. O how hap - py we will be, When from sor - row we are free,
4. At the bless - ed Sav-iour's feet, There a hap - py band we meet,
5. We will wan-der up and down, Thro' Im-man-uel's shin-ing ground,
When we all get home o - ver there; We shall nev-er know a sigh,
When we all get home o - ver there; In that nev-er end-ing day
When we all get home o - ver there; We will chant glad strains of love
When we all get home o - ver there; Of our tri-umphs we will tell
When we all get home o - ver there; Thro' a vast e - ter - ni - ty
D. S.—Fear can nev-er en - ter there
FINE.
In those mansions bright on high, When we all get home o - ver there.
Naught shall cloud the Lamb's pure ray, When we all get home o - ver there.
In that cit - y fair a-bove, When we all get home o - ver there.
While in love we sweetly dwell, When we all get home o - ver there.
Per - fect bliss our lot shall be, When we all get home o - ver there.
In those mansions bright and fair, When we all get home o - ver there.
CHORUS.
D.S.
When we all get home o-ver there, When we all get home o-ver there,
o-ver there, o-ver there,

Controlled by D. E. Dortch.

27. THE PRECIOUS NAME.

PRISCILLA J. OWENS. E. S. LORENZ.

1. One name shall echo through the world, When names of pride have perished, In
2. One name shall rise the strife a - bove, When battles all are end - ed; Shall
3. One name doth brighten all the past, Shall make the future glo-ry; The
light in-scribed, in tears impearled, O'er all beloved and cher-ished; O
float a - far on wings of love With an - gel cho-rus blend - ed. An -
roll - ing wave, the rushing blast, Shall spread its loving sto - ry. All
heav-enly ech - oes, soft-ly roll That name melodious through my soul,
gel - ic cho - rus, ev-er roll That name melodious through my soul,
lov - ing voi - ces join to roll That name melodious through my soul,
The dear-est name, the sweetest name, The precious name of Je - sus.
The dear-est name, the sweetest name, The precious name of Je - sus.
The dear-est name, the sweetest name, The precious name of Je - sus.

28. JOIN THE SONG.

MARK ADAMS. E. S. LORENZ.

1. Let us join the hap-py song which the morn - ing stars, Filled with
2. Let us join the sol-emn song of the hosts un - told, Long since
3. Let us join the song of life, sung by hosts a - bove, Who, once
won - der and de-light, In the world's fair morn-ing bright, Bring to
crum- bled in - to dust; Yet their praise re-vive we must, As his
vile in sin and base, Now be - hold the Fa-ther's face; 'Tis the
Him who rules on high, in mel - o-dious bars, And a- dore the Lord of might.
law of ho - ly truth- we a-gain be-hold, Let us praise the Lord so just.
grand-est song of heav'n, 'tis a song of love; Praise the Lord of wondrous grace.
CHORUS.
Join the song! Sing his praise with heart and voice! Join the song!
join the song! join the song!
With the hosts a-bove re-joice! For the Lord our God is great, he is

ev - er good and true; Un - to him our praise is due.

29. MUST I GO WITH EMPTY HANDS?

REV. J. H. MARTIN. E. HANKS.

1. { Must I go with emp - ty hands, When I leave this vale be-low?
When I reach ce - les - tial lands, Have no gleanings there to show? }
2. { Must I go with emp - ty hands, There to stand be-fore the throne?
Must I join the ran-somed bands, With no sheaves to call my own? }
CHORUS.
No, no, no, no, no, no, I'll work with a will - ing hand;
From morning till night, I'll labor with might, I'll obey the Lord's command.

3 Must I go with empty hands,
And appear before the King,
Where the heavenly temple stands,
Bearing him no offering?

4 Must I go with empty hands,
While the vast triumphant throng,
Souls redeemed from many lands,
Come with gifts and joyful songs?

30. THE GRACE OF GOD.

ESTELLE DAVISON. E. HANKS.

1. Oh, hast thou not heard of the prom - is - es sweet, That our
2. All his chil- dren in grace shall for - ev - er a-bound, And his
3. As the wom - an of old to the proph-et ap- peals, In the
Fa-ther hath giv - en to men; And dost thou not see in the
good-ness their needs will sup-ply; Se-cure in their faith not a
hour of her bit - ter-est need; They ask for the help that they
book of our God, They are writ - ten a - gain and a - gain?
fear can they know! To the Rock of Sal - va - tion they fly.
know will not fail, From the Friend ev - er read - y to heed.
CHORUS.
He is a - ble and will-ing to care for thee, Oh, be -
lieve in his word, trust him and come; And his love and his

rit.
grace will pre-pare for thee A home, beau - ti - ful home.

31. THE EDEN LAND.

JENNIE WILSON. W. J. BALTZELL.

1. There's an E - den land o'er the swelling tide, That breaks on the shores of time,
2. In the E - den land for the wea - ry waits, Sweet rest af - ter toil and strife,
3. In the E - den land dwell pure souls, redeemed, By Calva-ry's sac - ri - fice,
4. To that deathless land an - gel voic - es call Us o - ver the billow's foam,
And no sin or care ev - er en - ters there, To shad - ow that cloudless clime.
In its ho - ly calm comes the blessed balm, Of peace by the stream of life.
And in Je - sus' praise thro' e - ter - nal days, Their hymns of re-joic - ing rise.
And with joy un - told we shall soon be-hold, Our beau - ti - ful E - den home.
CHORUS.
O E - den land! love-ly E - den land, Land of beau - ty, glad and bright!
Soon our barks shall glide o'er the swelling tide, To thy happy ports of light.

32. LET YOUR LIGHT SO SHINE.

PRISCILLA J. OWENS. E. S. LORENZ.

1. Set the watch, trim the lamps, guard each station, Christian keepers, whose light
2. Keep your light thro' the night brightly burn-ing, Shin-ing warm to the soul
3. Let your light shine, the dark-ness o'er-flow-ing; All around you God's good
is sal-va-tion; Shine to cheer, and to warn in temp-ta-tion, While
far dis-cern-ing; Guid-ing homeward the wand'rers re-turn-ing, While
ness be showing; Keep your love and your faith ev-er glow-ing, While
CHORUS.
God makes glo-ry in the soul.
God makes glo-ry in your soul.
God makes glo-ry in the soul.
Let your light so shine, O my broth-er!
Glow with pow'r di-vine, O my brother! That the world may ev-er glo-ry,
As it reads sal-va-tion's sto-ry, In the light with which your life doth shine.

33. JESUS IS THE BLESSED NAME.

CHAS. H. GABRIEL. D. E. DORTCH.

1. There is a name so sweet to me, A name that charms my ear;
2. There is a voice so low and sweet, That oft - en speaks to me;
3. O, bles - sed name, O, hal-low'd voice, Di - rect me here be - low,
That bids my ach - ing heart re-joice, And gives my spir - it cheer.
My droop-ing soul it wakes, inspires, And helps me faith-ful be.
And when I die, oh, lead me home, From sin and grief and woe.
CHORUS.
Je - sus is the bles-sed name, bles-sed name, Je - sus
blessed name,
is the blessed name that I love; I will sing it while I've breath,
I will laud it e'en in death, Join the praise of hosts a-bove, hosts a-bove.

Controlled by D. E. Dortch.

34. IT DOTH NOT YET APPEAR.

E. H. E. HANKS.

1. It doth not yet ap-pear what we shall be, And we know not yet the
2. It doth not yet ap-pear what we shall be, And we know not yet the
3. It doth not yet ap-pear what we shall be, And we know not yet the
4. It doth not yet ap-pear what we shall be, And we know not yet the
countenance that we shall wear; But we know that when the Lord shall
glo - ries of our man-sions fair; But we know that we shall go with
rap-ture of the mu - sic sweet; But we know that we shall strike the
beau-ties we shall there unfold; But we know that we'll be more than
D. S.—But we know that when the Lord shall
FINE.
come a - gain, We shall see him as he is and his im - age bear.
him to dwell, In that cit - y of pure gold and its bless - ing share.
gold - en lyre, And shall sing with kindred dear at the Sav - iour's feet.
sat - is - fied When we en-ter through the gates of those courts of gold.
come a - gain, We shall see him as he is, and his im - age bear.
CHORUS.
D. S.
Be - lov-ed, now are we the sons of God, What we shall be doth not yet appear;

35. I WILL COME TO THEE.

REV. M. LOWRIE HOFFORD. E. S. LORENZ.

1. Sav-iour in the morn-ing I will come to thee; Low - ly at thy
2. Sav-iour at the noon-day I will draw a-side From life's act-ive
3. Sav-iour in the eve - ning, When the shadows fall And the heart is
foot - stool I will bend the knee. Wait-ing for thy bless-ing
du - ties, Near - er to thy side, And de - vout - ly wait-ing
ten - der On thy name I'll call; Thankful for thy good-ness
D. S.—Heark - en, bless - ed Sav - iour,
Fine.
Thro' the coming day, Trust-ing in thy mer - cy I will kneel and pray.
Will my strength renew For the rug-ged paths that dai - ly I pur-sue.
Thro' the passing day, Humbly at thy foot-stool I will kneel and pray.
Our pe - ti - tion hear, Fill our souls with glad-ness And our hearts with cheer.
Chorus.
Pray - ing, Plead - ing prom - ise sweet,
bless - ed Sav - iour,
D. S.
Hear us, Fall - ing at thy feet;
bless - ed Sav - iour,

36. ARE YOU FOR JESUS?

EDEN R. LATTA. E. S. LORENZ.

1. Are you for Je-sus? ex-press it! Tell it to-day! Tell it to-day!
2. Are you for Je-sus? don't hide it! Tell it to-day! Tell it to-day!
3. Are you for Je-sus? re-veal it! Tell it to-day! Tell it to-day!
Be not ashamed to con-fess it, Tell it to-day, to-day!
What if the world should deride it? Tell it to-day, to-day!
Why should you seek to con-ceal it? Tell it to-day, to-day!
Have you your fol-lies for-sak-en? Tell it, tell it to-day!
Are you 'gainst e-vil con-tend-ing? Tell it, tell it to-day!
Does the Re-deem-er con-fess you? Tell it, tell it to-day!
Tru-ly his cross have you ta-ken? Tell it, tell it to-day!
Are you on Je-sus de-pend-ing? Tell it, tell it to-day!
Does he for-give you and bless you? Tell it, tell it to-day!
CHORUS.
Tell it to-day, for the Master will hear! Tell it to-day, for our hearts it will cheer!

ARE YOU FOR JESUS? Concluded.

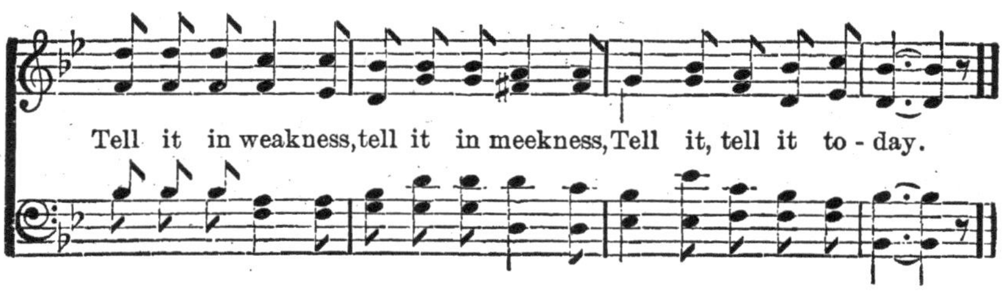
Tell it in weakness, tell it in meekness, Tell it, tell it to - day.

37. CORONATION.

EDWARD PERRONET. OLIVER HOLDEN.

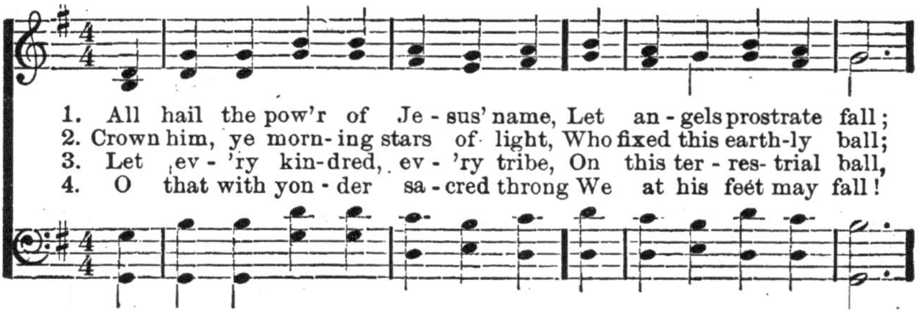
1. All hail the pow'r of Je - sus' name, Let an - gels prostrate fall;
2. Crown him, ye morn - ing stars of light, Who fixed this earth - ly ball;
3. Let ev - 'ry kin - dred, ev - 'ry tribe, On this ter - res - trial ball,
4. O that with yon - der sa - cred throng We at his feet may fall!

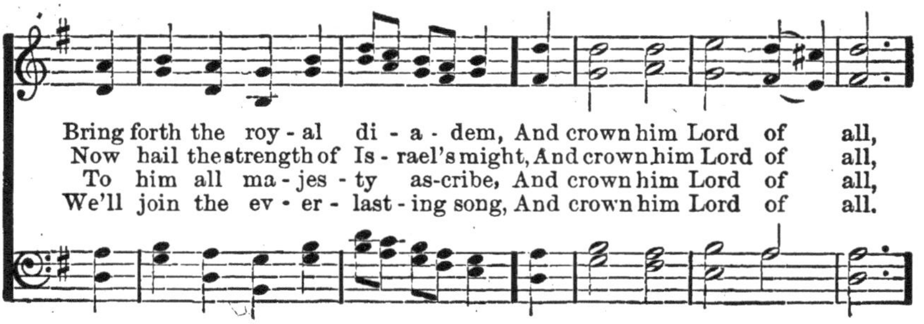
Bring forth the roy - al di - a - dem, And crown him Lord of all,
Now hail the strength of Is - rael's might, And crown him Lord of all,
To him all ma - jes - ty as - cribe, And crown him Lord of all,
We'll join the ev - er - last - ing song, And crown him Lord of all.

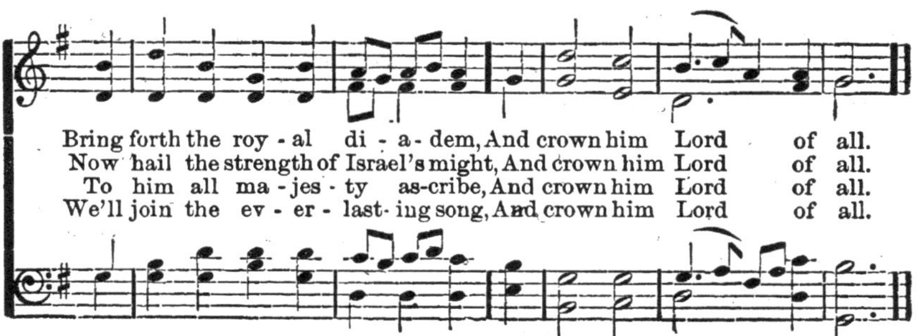
Bring forth the roy - al di - a - dem, And crown him Lord of all.
Now hail the strength of Israel's might, And crown him Lord of all.
To him all ma - jes - ty as - cribe, And crown him Lord of all.
We'll join the ev - er - last - ing song, And crown him Lord of all.

38. COME SING TO ME OF JESUS' LOVE.

REV. BEN. HELM. EDW. S. FOGG.

1. Come sing to me of Je-sus' love, For life's low tide is ebb-ing fast;
2. Draw near and soft-ly sing to me, How then on him my sins are laid,
3. Oh, sing a-gain of Cal-va-ry, Where Je-sus died my soul to save;
4. Sing how, tho' now ex-alt-ed high, At his Almight-y Father's side,
Sing how he came from heav'n above, How with lost men his lot he cast.
That I now in his cross may see That all my debt is ful-ly paid.
Yea, sing the glorious mys-ter-y, Of how he triumph'd o'er the grave.
In death's lone wave he still is nigh, To bear me safe-ly o'er the tide.
CHORUS.
Sing of his love, ... his won-der-ful love,
Sing of his love, his wonder-ful love,
How that he died, ... on Calv'ry for me,
How that he died on Calv'ry for me;
Sing of his love, ... His wonder-ful love,
Sing of his love, His won-der-ful love,

Controlled by D. E. Dortch.

COME SING TO ME OF JESUS' LOVE. Concluded.

How that he died, ... for you and for me,
How that he died for you and for me.

39. YOUNG MEN AND MAIDENS.

E. D. MUND. E. S. LORENZ.

CHORUS.

Young men and maid-ens, Praise ye the Lord! Num - ber-less bless-ings On you hath he poured.
1. For the life your puls - es thrill-ing, For the hope glad hearts now filling, Praise the Lord! oh, praise the Lord!
2. For the hand that ev - er guides you, For the rock that safe-ly hides you, Praise the Lord! oh, praise the Lord!
3. For the love your path-way brightens, All your heav- y burdens lightens, Praise the Lord! oh, praise the Lord!
4. For the good that waits your do - ing, No - ble ends for your pur- su- ing, Praise the Lord! oh, praise the Lord!
5. For your in - fluence still immor - tal When you pass heav'n's shining portal, Praise the Lord! oh, praise the Lord!

40. WHY STAND YE HERE IDLE?

E. R. LATTA. D. E. DORTCH.

1. Why stand ye here i - dle, with so much to do? The
2. Why stand ye here i - dle the whole of the day? The
3. Why stand ye here i - dle, when great is the need? To
har - vest un - gath-ered, all round ye may view! The Mas - ter your
mo-ments are pass - ing with swift-ness a - way! The lab'-rers are
gath - er the har - vest, or scat - ter the seed? Go work for the
la - bor will ful - ly re-quite! Go toil in his vine-yard from
glean-ing the sheaves of bright grain! Oh, has - ten to join them, or
Sav - iour with heart and with hand, No long - er be will - ing thus
CHORUS.
morn - ing till night.
soon 'twill be vain.
i - dle to stand.
Do much or do lit - tle, still toil with your
might! Go work for the Mas - ter, from morn - ing till night.

41. FOR CHRIST AND THE CHURCH.

W. F. M. W. F. McCAULEY.

With spirit.
1. For Christ and the Church our songs we raise, A cho - rus full and free,
2. We come to work at his command And spread his truth a - broad.
3. We con - se - crate our feeble pow'rs, And lay them at his feet,
For Christ and the Church u - nite our praise, The notes of ju - bi - lee.
Re - ceiv - ing from his own right hand The pan - o - ply of God.
And pray that cour - age may be ours For ev - 'ry ser - vice meet.
CHORUS.
For Christ we sing A cho - rus full and free.
For Christ and the Church we sing, we sing,
For Christ we bring The notes of ju - bi - lee.
For Christ and the Church we bring, we bring

42. DAY BY DAY.

E. D. MUND. E. S. LORENZ.

1. { By the grace of God renewed, Day by day, day by day; }
{ Filled with life's rich plen - ti - tude, Day by day, day by day. }
2. { What tho' fierce temp-ta-tion come, Day by day, day by day? }
{ What tho' life's cold blasts be-numb, Day by day, day by day? }
3. { On our way we up-ward press, Day by day, day by day; }
{ Brave - ly meet-ing pain, dis-tress, Day by day, day by day; }
Struggling, stumb-ling, oft cast down, Forced our weakness still to own,
God will nev - er leave his own, Round them still his arm is thrown;
For each tri - al strength is giv'n, Thro' each rock a path is riv'n,
God his help has ev - er shown, Day by day, day by day.
He it is who stills each moan, Day by day, day by day.
God leads on-ward near-er heav'n, Day by day, day by day.
CHORUS.
Day by day the way grows brighter, Day by day the bur-den light-er;
Grace to live God will give Day by day, day by day.

43. WHAT WONDROUS LOVE.

ANON. ARR. BY D. E. DORTCH.

1. What wondrous love is this,—O my soul! O my soul! What
2. When I was sink-ing down, Sink-ing down, sink-ing down, When
3. Ye wing-ed ser-aphs, fly! Bear the news! bear the news! Ye
4. To God and to the Lamb I will sing! I will sing! To
wondrous love is this,—O my soul! What wondrous love is this
I was sink-ing down, Sink-ing down! When I was sink-ing down
wing-ed ser-aphs, fly, Bear the news! Ye wing-ed ser-aphs, fly
God and to the Lamb I will sing! To God and to the Lamb,
That caused the Lord of bliss To bear the dread-ful curse For my
Be-neath God's righteous frown, Christ laid a-side his crown For my
Like light-ning thro' the sky, Fill vast e-ter-ni-ty With the
And to the great I Am, While mil-lions join the psalm, I will
soul, for my soul? To bear the dread-ful curse For my soul?
soul, for my soul; Christ laid a-side his crown For my soul.
news, with the news, Fill vast e-ter-ni-ty With the news.
sing, I will sing, While mil-lions join the psalm, I will sing!

44. OVER JORDAN WE SHALL MEET.

W. T. DALE. D. E. DORTCH.

1. O - ver Jor-dan we shall meet, By and by, by and by, In that
2. All our sor-rows shall be past, By and by, by and by, We shall
3. We shall join the heav'nly choir, By and by, by and by, We shall
4. There we'll join the ransom'd throng, By and by, by and by, Chant-ing
hap-py land so sweet, By and by; We shall gath-er on the shore, With our
reach our home at last, By and by; With the ransom'd we shall stand, There a
strike the gold-en lyre, By and by; In our home so bright and fair, Where the
love's redemption song, By and by; There we'll meet before the throne, There we'll
kindred gone be-fore, And the Sav-iour's name a - dore, By and by.
ho - ly, hap - py band, Crown'd with glory in that land, By and by.
hap-py an- gels are, We shall praise for - ev - er there, By and by.
lay our trophies down, And re-ceive a shin - ing crown, By and by.
CHORUS.
By and by, by and by, O-ver Jor-dan we shall
By and by, By and by,

OVER JORDAN WE SHALL MEET. Concluded.

gath-er, by and by; by and by; By and by, by and by, by and
by, by and by, Then we'll shout and sing forev-er, by and by, by and by.

45. LABAN.

GEO. HEATH. DR. L. MASON.

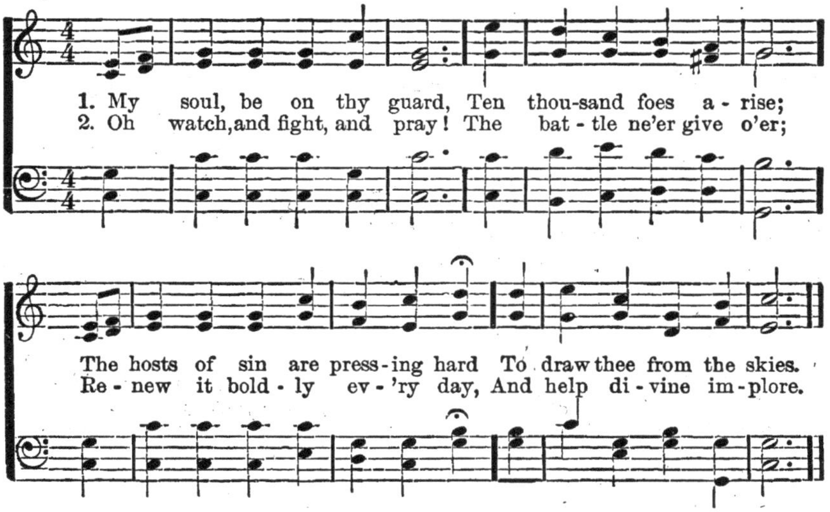
1. My soul, be on thy guard, Ten thou-sand foes a-rise;
2. Oh watch, and fight, and pray! The bat-tle ne'er give o'er;
The hosts of sin are press-ing hard To draw thee from the skies.
Re-new it bold-ly ev-'ry day, And help di-vine im-plore.

3 Ne'er think the victory won,
Nor lay thine armor down;
Thy arduous work will not be done
Till thou obtain thy crown.

4 Fight on, my soul, till death
Shall bring thee to thy God!
He'll take thee at thy parting breath
To his divine abode.

46. "A CUP OF WATER."

WM. HENRY GARDNER. E. S. LORENZ.

1. If 'tis but a cup of wa-ter, Giv-en in the Mas-ter's name,
2. Just a lit-tle word of com-fort, Spo-ken to some fainting heart,
3. One sweet smile of kind-ly wel-come, Flashed in-to a stranger's face,
4. If 'tis love that prompts the ac-tion, It will ev-er bless-ed be.
Yet the deed the Sav-iour pleas-eth, Though it can no greatness claim.
Yet the Sav-iour loves the speak-er, Do-ing thus her lit-tle part.
Makes the drear-y way look brighter, Fills his heart with ho-ly grace.
Je-sus knows each ten-der long-ing, He the in-most heart doth see.
CHORUS.
On-ly a cup of wa-ter, Giv-en some wea-ry one;
Yet Christ will say, Some hap-py day, "O faith-ful soul, well done!"

47. JESUS WILL FORGIVE.

REV. J. H. MARTIN. D. E. DORTCH.

1. Art thou burdened with thy sin? Is there deep un-rest with-in?
2. Is thy soul oppressed with gloom? With the dread of wrath and doom?
3. Come to Him with all thy stain, He will cleanse thee, soothe thy pain;
4. On his pre-cious prom-ise rest, Lean by faith up-on his breast,
Wouldst thou pardon, peace, receive? Confess thy sins and Jesus will for-give.
Long-ing to es-cape and live? Confess thy sins and Jesus will for-give.
On the Son of God be-lieve, Confess thy sins and Jesus will for-give.
He will all thy woes re-lieve, Confess thy sins and Jesus will for-give.
REFRAIN.
Je-sus will for-give, Je-sus will for-give, Con-fess thy sins and Je-sus will for-give; Je-sus will for-give,
Rit.
Je-sus will for-give, Con-fess thy sins and Je-sus will for-give.

48. OPEN ARMS OF JESUS.

E. D. MUND. | E. S. LORENZ.

1. O-pen are the arms of Je-sus, Re-fuge for a dy-ing race;
2. O-pen are the arms of Je-sus, Love is beam-ing from his eye;
3. Safe with-in the arms of Je-sus, All the world may storm and rage;
4. O-pen are the arms of Je-sus, Love's de-light-ful hid-ing place;
Oh what love, what ten-der pit-y, That afford such wondrous grace.
He will shel-ter, he will cher-ish, All who to his bos-om fly.
Strong his arm is to de-liv-er From the foes our souls en-gage.
Who can speak the joy, the rap-ture, Of the soul in his embrace.
CHORUS.
Lov-ing arms of Je-sus, hid-ing place for me,
Ref-uge in temp-ta-tion, whith-er I may flee;
Ev-er may the arms of Je-sus Ten-der-ly en-cir-cle me.

49. TILL WE MEET AGAIN.

JENNIE WILSON. D. E. DORTCH.

1. May the love of God be with you, Un-til we a-gain shall meet,
2. May the love of God be with you, Whate'er path your feet may tread,
3. May the love of God be with you, Thro' the flight of ev-'ry hour,
4. May the love of God be with you, Till your journey's sol-emn end,
Strength and guidance may he give you, And his con-so-la-tion sweet.
May you thro' the light or shad-ow Ten-der-ly by him be led.
Sanc-ti-fy-ing grief or glad-ness By its sweet and sa-cred pow'r.
Where the words of earth-ly part-ings With an-gel-ic wel-come blend.
CHORUS.
Till we meet a-gain, till we meet a-gain, Till we meet on life's sunny shore,
May the love of God, may the love of God Guard and keep you all ev-er-more.

50. SOWING THE TARES.

Words by a "Convict." CHAS. EDW. POLLOCK.

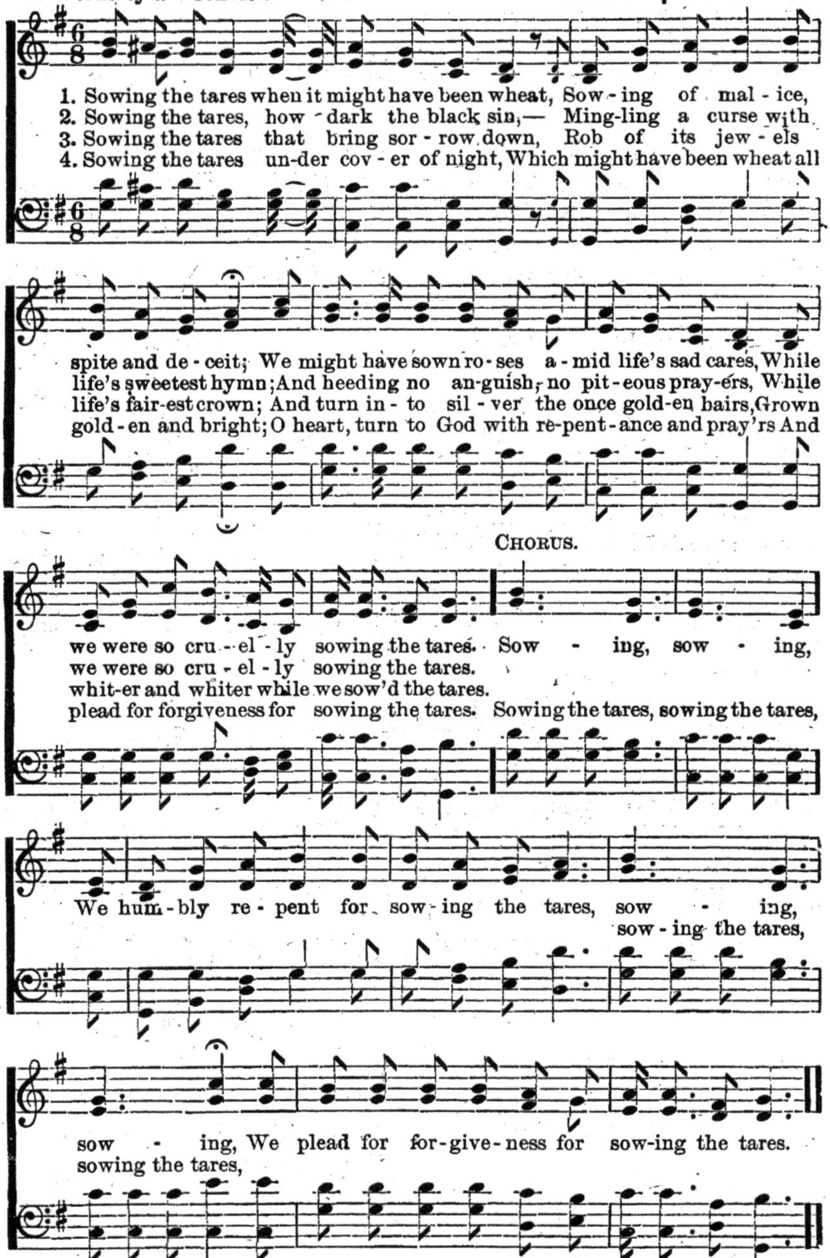
1. Sowing the tares when it might have been wheat, Sow-ing of mal-ice,
2. Sowing the tares, how dark the black sin,— Ming-ling a curse with
3. Sowing the tares that bring sor-row down, Rob of its jew-els
4. Sowing the tares un-der cov-er of night, Which might have been wheat all
spite and de-ceit; We might have sown ro-ses a-mid life's sad cares, While
life's sweetest hymn; And heeding no an-guish, no pit-eous pray-ers, While
life's fair-est crown; And turn in-to sil-ver the once gold-en hairs, Grown
gold-en and bright; O heart, turn to God with re-pent-ance and pray'rs And
CHORUS.
we were so cru-el-ly sowing the tares. Sow-ing, sow-ing,
we were so cru-el-ly sowing the tares.
whit-er and whiter while we sow'd the tares.
plead for forgiveness for sowing the tares. Sowing the tares, sowing the tares,
We hum-bly re-pent for sow-ing the tares, sow-ing,
sow-ing the tares,
sow-ing, We plead for for-give-ness for sow-ing the tares.
sowing the tares,

By permission of C. E. Pollock.

51. TRUSTING ONLY THEE.

FRANCES R. HAVERGAL. E. S. LORENZ.

1. I am trust-ing thee, dear Sav-iour, Trust-ing on-ly thee;
2. I am trust-ing thee for par-don, At thy feet I bow;
3. I am trust-ing thee for cleans-ing In the crim-son flood;
4. I am trust-ing thee, Lord Je-sus, Nev-er let me fall;
Trust-ing thee for full sal-va-tion, Oh, how great and free!
For thy grace and ten-der mer-cy I am trust-ing now.
Trust-ing thee to make me ho-ly By thy pre-cious blood.
I am trust-ing thee for ev-er, Trust-ing thee for all.
CHORUS.
Trust-ing thee, tho' dark-ness fall, tho' dark-ness fall; Trust-ing
thee, tho' sins ap-pall, tho' sins ap-pall; Trust-ing
thee, I con-quer all, I con-quer all, Trust-ing on-ly thee.

52. HEAR THE SAVIOUR CALLING.

E. S. F. E. S. FOGG.

1. When I was far a - way from God, And all was dark to me,
2. Yet still I wander'd on in sin, Still world-ly pleas-ures sought,
3. But in my hopeless- ness that voice Was speaking love e'en then,
4. And now that I this new birth have, And God lives in my soul,
I heard a voice from heav-en say, "The Sav-iour calls for thee.
Un - til it seemed all hope had fled, I had my ru - in wrought.
"If thou would'st full sal - va- tion have, Thou must be born a - gain."
I pray you sin - ner turn to Christ, That he may make you whole.
Chorus.
He's calling for thee, ... oh, sin-ner o - bey, ... The
He's calling for thee, oh, sin-ner o - bey,
Saviour still pleads, ... he's pleading to- day, ... Oh,
The Saviour still pleads, he's pleading to-day,
hear his sweet voice, ... and turn not a - way, ... For
Oh, hear his sweet voice, and turn not away,

Controlled by D. E. Dortch.

Je - sus is wait - - - - - ing to save you to - day.
For Je - sus is wait-ing

53. WILL FOLLOW HIM.

PRISCILLA J. OWENS. JOHN TIBBALLS.

1. Turn thy steps from earth's flatt'ring throng, Fol - low the Sav - iour;
2. All thy sor - rows Je - sus has known, Fol - low the Sav - iour;
3. Dark - ness falls and death's night is near, Fol - low the Sav - iour;
Trust his love to guide thee a - long, Hold fast his word.
Hear his voice, you walk not a - lone, Hold fast his word.
Close to him you need nev - er fear; Hold fast his word.
CHORUS.
We'll fol - low him, his cross upbearing; We'll fol - low him, his sor - row sharing;
For him all pain and dan - ger bearing, We'll fol - low the Lord.

54. WAITING IN THE BORDERLAND.

Words and Melody by
MRS. LAURA E. NEWELL.

Harmonized by
C. K. LANGLEY.

SOLO. Legato.
1. I'm wait - ing in the bor - der-land, While sun-set tints the skies,
2. I'm wait - ing in the bor - der-land, Tho' friends I love the best
3. I'm wait - ing in the bor - der-land, My mor - tal strength may fail;
And soon my soul shall un - der-stand The bliss of Par - a - dise, . . .
Have join'd the hap - py ran-somed band, And dwell a-mong the blest. . .
But e - ven now my brow is fanned By E - den's gen - tle gale. . .
For He is walk-ing by my side, Who walk'd up-on the sea; . . In
But I have nev - er walked a-lone, A friend has clung to me, . . Whose
Dear hands are beck'ning me to come, And Je - sus leads the way, . . To
his blest love I still a - bide,—My Sav - iour lead - eth me. . .
love and peace for all a - tone, His face I soon shall see. . .
yon - der bet - ter, heav - 'nly home, Where bides e - ter - nal day. . .
REFRAIN.
all the way, . . .
I'm wait - ing in the bor - der-land, Yet clear - er, clear - er all the way;

WAITING IN THE BORDERLAND. Concluded.

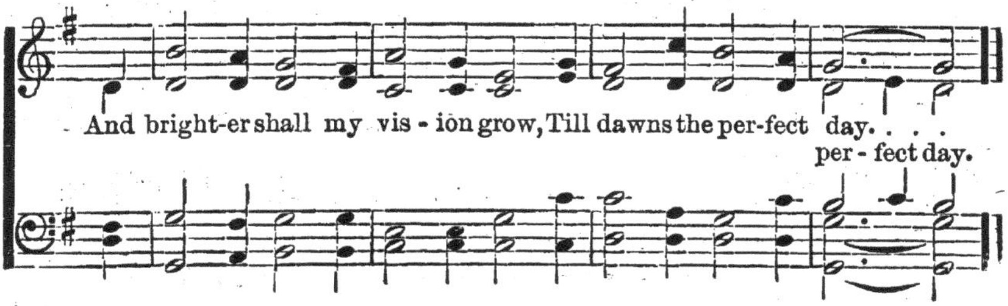
And bright-er shall my vis - ion grow, Till dawns the per-fect day. . . .
per - fect day.

55. WHEN THE SHADOWS FLEE AWAY.

WM. H. GARDNER. E. S. LORENZ.

1. There will be a fair - er dawn-ing, There will be a bright-er day,
2. There will be an end of sad-ness, And our wea - ry hearts can say,
3. There will be no dear ones part-ed, On that sweet and hap - py day,
4. Hap - py hearts will all be sing-ing, Thro' the long e - ter - nal day,
On that hap - py gold - en morn-ing, When the shad - ows flee a - way.
We shall taste the wine of glad-ness, When the shad - ows flee a - way.
Christ will heal the bro - ken heart-ed, When the shad - ows flee a - way.
Loud hos - an - nas will be ring - ing, When the shad - ows flee a - way.
CHORUS.
When the shad - ows flee a - way, Joy will come, joy will come!
When the shad - ows flee a - way, Joy will come.

56. SOWING, EVER SOWING.

E. R. LATTA. J. M. HOGAN.
Arr. by D. E. Dortch.

1. We are sow - ing, ev-er sow - ing, In the paths where others move;
2. We are sow - ing, ev-er sow - ing, Be the weath - er foul or fair;
3. We are sow - ing, ev-er sow - ing, In the home and on the street;
And the har - vest that shall follow, Shall a bane or blessing prove;
Heed-less-ly how oft we scat-ter, Where there's need of greatest care;
Sow-ing good or sow-ing e - vil, For our-selves and all we meet;
Are we sow - ing thorns and thistles, That shall pierce the trav'ler's feet;
Now's the seed - time, full of prom-ise, Full of pos - si - bil - i - ty;
Let us ear - nest-ly en-deav - or, Seeds of hap - pi - ness to strew;
Or the seeds of love and mer-cy, That shall make existence sweet?
What the fruit - age we shall gather, Here and in e - ter - ni - ty?
That our fel - low men may bless us, Where-so-ev - er we may go.
CHORUS.
Sow - ing pain or sow - ing pleas - ure,
Sow - ing pain or sow - ing pleas-ure, Sow-ing pain or sow - ing pleas-ure,

Controlled by D. E. Dortch.

SOWING, EVER SOWING. Concluded.

Sow - ing tares or gol - den wheat;
Sow - ing tares or gold-en wheat, yes, Sow-ing tares or gold - en wheat;
What, oh, what shall be the har - vest,
What, oh, what shall be the har-vest, what, oh what shall be the har-vest,
When our sow - ing is com-plete, yes, is com-plete?
When our sow-ing, when our sow-ing is com-plete, yes, is com-plete?

57. ROCK OF AGES.

AUGUSTUS M. TOPLADY. THOMAS HASTINGS.

FINE.
1. Rock of a - ges, cleft for me! Let me hide my - self in thee;
D. C.—*Be of sin the doub - le cure; Save from wrath and make me pure.*
D. C.
Let the wa - ter and the blood, From thy side a heal - ing flood,

2 Should my tears forever flow,
Should my zeal no languor know,
All for sin could not atone;
Thou must save, and thou alone;
In my hand no price I bring;
Simply to thy cross I cling.

3 While I draw this fleeting breath,
When mine eyelids close in death,
When I rise to worlds unknown,
See thee on thy judgment throne—
Rock of Ages, cleft for me,
Let me hide myself in thee.

58. THE BLESSED BIBLE.

E. D. MUND. E. S. LORENZ.

1. 'Tis a lamp un - to my feet, The bless-ed Bi - ble; On my way a guide complete, The blessed Bi - ble, When my soul would blindly stray, It re - veals the gold - en way, Lead-ing on to end - less day, The bless - ed Bi - ble.
2. 'Tis a treas - ure rich and vast, The bless-ed Bi - ble; And for aye its wealth will last, The blessed Bi - ble; Oth - er treasures fade and fail, All their joy and glo - ry pale, But this treas - ure will pre - vail, The bless - ed Bi - ble.
3. 'Tis rich food un - to my soul, The bless-ed Bi - ble; It will strengthen, make me whole, The blessed Bi - ble; On its prom-is - es I feed; In my sor - est want and need 'Tis the bread of life in-deed, This bless - ed Bi - ble.
CHORUS.
Bless - ed Bi - - ble, how I love it,
Hold no oth - - - er book a -
Bless-ed Bi - ble, how I love it, Bless - ed Bi - ble, how I love it, Hold no oth - er book a - bove it, Hold no

THE BLESSED BIBLE. Concluded.

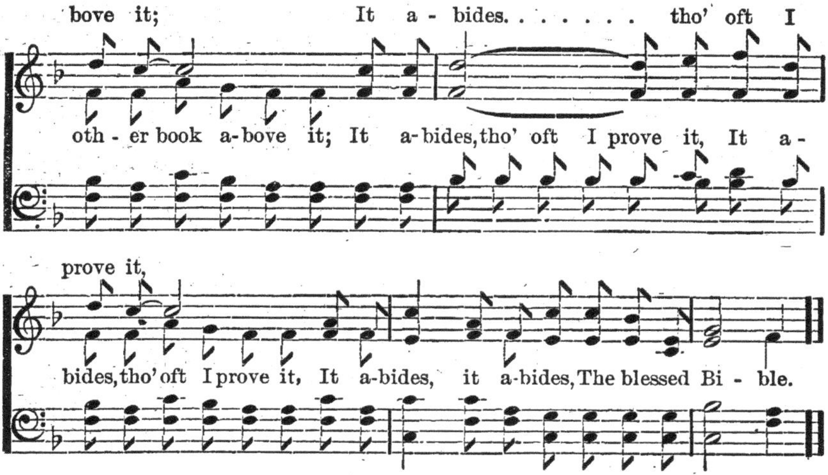
bove it; It a - bides. . . . . . . tho' oft I
oth - er book a - bove it; It a - bides, tho' oft I prove it, It a -
prove it,
bides, tho' oft I prove it, It a - bides, it a - bides, The blessed Bi - ble.

59. REMEMBER ME.

(Male Voices.)

ANON.

JOANNA KINKEL.

1. When storms a - round are sweeping, When lone my watch I'm keep - ing,
2. When walk - ing on life's o - cean, Con - trol its rag - ing mo - tion;
3. When weight of sin op - press - es, When dark des - pair dis - tress - es,
'Mid fires of e - vil fall - ing, 'Mid temp - ters' voic - es call - ing,
When from its dan - gers shrink - ing, When in its dread deeps sink - ing,
All thro' the life that's mor - tal, And when I pass death's por - tal,
CHORUS.
Re - member me, O Mighty One! Re - member me, O Might - y One.

60. I AM RESTING IN THE SAVIOUR'S LOVE.

REV. E. A. HOFFMAN. D. E. DORTCH.

1. Oh! my heart is thrill'd with wond'rous joy to - day, I am
2. All the doubts are van-ished, all my fears are gone, I am
3. O the bliss and rap-ture! O the wond-'rous peace! I am
4. So I live re - joic-ing in his love each day, I am
rest-ing in the Sav-iour's love; Christ, the Lord, has ta - ken all my
rest-ing in the Sav-iour's love; When I trust - ed Je - sus, lo! the
rest-ing in the Sav-iour's love; I have nev - er known so pure a
rest-ing in the Sav-iour's love; I am walk - ing with him in the
sins a - way, I am rest-ing in the Sav-iour's love.
work was done, I am rest-ing in the Sav-iour's love.
joy as this, I am rest-ing in the Sav-iour's love.
nar - row way, I am rest-ing in the Sav-iour's love.
REFRAIN.
I am resting, sweet - ly resting, I am resting in the Saviour's love;
rest-ing sweetly,

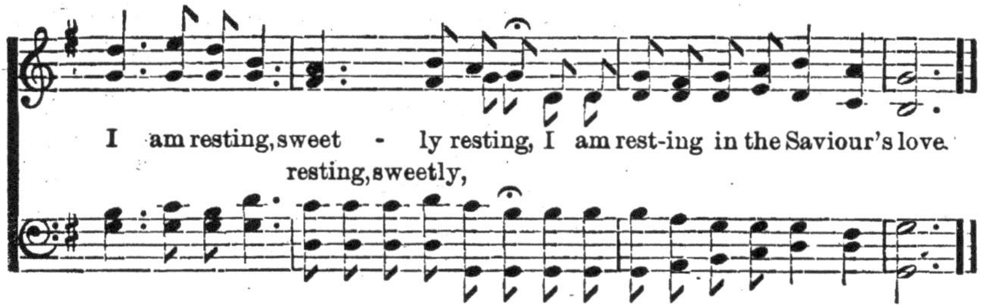
I am resting, sweet - ly resting, I am rest-ing in the Saviour's love.
resting, sweetly,

61. THOU THINKEST, LORD, OF ME.

E. D. MUND. E. S. LORENZ.

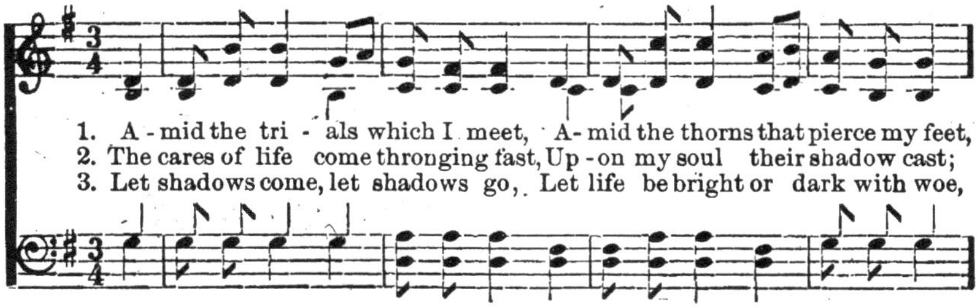
1. A - mid the tri - als which I meet, A- mid the thorns that pierce my feet,
2. The cares of life come thronging fast, Up - on my soul their shadow cast;
3. Let shadows come, let shadows go, Let life be bright or dark with woe,

FINE.
One thought remains su - preme - ly sweet, Thou thinkest, Lord, of me!
Their gloom re-minds my heart at last, Thou thinkest, Lord, of me!
I am con-tent, for this I know, Thou thinkest, Lord, of me!
D. S.—What need I fear when thou art near, And think-est, Lord, of me.

CHORUS.
D.S.
Thou think-est, Lord, of me, Thou thinkest, Lord, of me,
of me, of me,

62. THE TEMPLE OF PRAYER.

JESSIE H. BROWN. E. S. LORENZ.

1. At the wondrous temple whose name is Answer'd Pray'r, Ask, seek, and knock!
2. At thy first pe - ti - tion the gate may not swing wide; Ask, seek, and knock!
3. Still the promised an-swer may not at once ap-pear; Ask, seek, and knock!
Ask, seek, and knock! Promis'd boons of bless-ing a - wait thy entrance there,
Ask, seek, and knock! Seek with fervent long-ing that will not be de - nied—
Ask, seek, and knock! Knock, till thy beseech-ing shall reach the Father's ear;—
CHORUS.
Ask, at the Tem - ple of Pray'r.
Seek, at the Tem - ple of Pray'r.
Knock, at the Tem - ple of Pray'r.
Stand in ex - pec - ta - tion be - fore the tem-ple gate, Cast-ing from thy life ev - 'ry care;
Asking, seeking, knocking, in faith and patience wait, Wait at the Temple of Pray'r.

63. BUILDING ON THE ROCK.

D. E. DORTCH. D. E. DORTCH.

1. On the sol - id Rock I am build - ing, And my home will
2. On the sol - id Rock I am build - ing; Pre-cious stones, gold,
3. On the sol - id Rock I am build - ing; Wood and hay and
4. On the sol - id Rock I am build - ing, And my work will
5. O my broth-er, where are you build - ing, Is your house up -
sure-ly stand the storm; Tho' the tempest rage fierce and mad - ly, All is
sil-ver, may all be That I place each day in the tem - ple, I am
stub-ble will not stand For the fires of God will de-stroy them, His ap -
sure-ly there a - bide; Then the Lord will say, Faith-ful ser-vant, A re -
on the Rock, or sand? When the winds and waves beat up-on it, Will it
D. S.— On the sol - id Rock I am build-ing, And my
Chorus.
safe, for it can do no harm.
build-ing for e - ter - ni - ty.
prov - al they can ne'er command.
ward a-waits you by my side.
fall in wreck, or will it stand?
On the sol - id Rock is my
house will sure - ly stand the storm.
D. S.
build-ing sure, Tho' the tem - pest shock, still it is se - cure.

Controlled by D. E. Dortch.

5. Round Notes.

64. THE HARBOR IN SIGHT.

P. J. O. E. S. LORENZ.

SOLO.
1. What tow'rs are those that rise A - bove the mists of death?
2. What groves are those that bend A - bove the wa - ters clear?
3. 'Tis Je - sus calls, "A - rise, Come and go hence with me;
4. A - bove the sil - ver waves Sweet kin - dred fa - ces shine;
What splen-dor greets my fad - ing eyes, And thrills my fail - ing breath?
What voice of mu - sic comes to send, Its greet - ing to my ear?
Fear not to lift thy fail - ing eyes, My glo - ry thou shalt see."
Now fare-well, earth, thou land of graves, E - ter - nal life is mine.
QUARTETTE.
The beau - ti - ful har - bor comes in sight A - cross the bil - lows foam;
It throws a - far a glit-ter - ing light, A wel-come, welcome home!
welcome home!
It throws a - far a glit-t'ring light, A wel-come, wel-come home.

65. JESUS IS WAITING.

MRS. C. L. SHACKLOCK. D. E. DORTCH.

1. Wand-ring and wea - ry, O why dost thou stray! Come to the
2. Come then, be - lieve him, for he is the truth; Just now re -
3. Hearts that are bro - ken by him are made whole; He is the
Sav - iour for he is the Way; Friend-less and home-less, O
ceive him, in age or in youth; Come for the ran - som al -
life and the light of the soul; Grace all suf - fi-cient he
why wilt thou roam? Je - sus is wait - ing to wel-come thee home.
read - y is paid; He hath redeemed thee, a - tone-ment is made.
of - fers to thee; Come, for his mer - cy is boundless and free.
CHORUS.
Je - sus is wait - ing, Je - sus is wait - ing,
Je - sus is wait - ing to wel - come thee home.

Controlled by D. E. Dortch.

66. IN NEWNESS OF LIFE.

JENNIE WILSON. D. E. DORTCH.

1. Walk-ing with Je-sus in newness of life, Trust-ing him day by day,
2. Rest for the wea-ry and strength for the weak, In the new life is found;
3. Newness of life brings us promis-es sweet, Hopes that ex-tend past time,
4. Praise be to God for his in-fin-ite love, Praise for his cleansing pow'r,
Trav-el-ing homeward 'mid sor-row and strife, Tread we the nar-row way.
Close to our lov-ing Lord ho-ly and meek, Gladness and peace a-bound.
Hopes that will have the fru-i-tion complete Found in the land sub-lime.
Fit-ting our souls for his pure home above, Keep-ing us safe each hour.
CHORUS.
Walk-ing in new-ness of life how blest! Knowing our sins for-giv'n;
Sweet-ly in Christ's saving love we can rest, Jour-ney-ing home to heav'n.

67. LOVE IS KING.

H. F. JAMES. E. S. LORENZ.

1. Faith is might - y, vic - to - ry giv - ing, And Hope a bless - ed
2. Love is King! O mes-sage so ten - der, That moves the wings of
3. Love is King! and glad - ly we're yielding Our hearts to his be -
com - fort can bring; O'er them all, a - dored by all liv - ing, Sits
an - gels on high; Glad they haste o - be - dience to ren - der, And
nef - i - cent sway; In our lives the sole pow - er wield - ing, O
Love enthron'd, for Love is the King!
quick - ly on Love's er - rand they fly.
may he there his glo - ry dis - play.
CHORUS,
Yes, Love is King in
earth and heav - en! To Love, the King, the crown is giv - en; To
him we yield That we may wield The pow'r of Love, for Love is the King!

STEP IN THE LIFE-BOAT.

PERLA E. HIGGINS. D. E. DORTCH.

1. The life - boat is launch'd on the wild, stormy sea, To res - cue the
2. The life - boat is launch'd, it is now at your side; Christ's hands are out -
3. The life - boat is launch'd, she is tak-ing us home, While thousands are
lost who are drift - ing a-way; For Sa - tan is striv-ing their
stretch'd to af - ford you re-lief; Ac - cept the kind aid and be
drift - ing to end - less de-spair; O, broth - er, come with us, sal -
Rit.
souls to ob-tain, Yes, Je - sus is call - ing, "I'll save you to-day."
rescued from death; Re - ject - ing is choos-ing your soul's end - less grief.
- va-tion is free; The Sav-iour will par - don, sub - mit to his care.
Chorus.
Step in the life-boat, step in the life-boat, Jesus invites you, no long-er de-lay;
Rit.
Step in the life-boat, step in the life-boat, Je-sus is calling, "I'll save you to-day."

69. WONDERFUL GOSPEL.

ANNA CHICHESTER. E. S. LORENZ.

1. Won-der-ful gos-pel of Je - sus! Won-der-ful message of peace!
2. Won-der-ful gos-pel of Je - sus, Hearts once despairing now hope;
3. Won-der-ful gos-pel of Je - sus, Heal-ing the broken in heart;
4. Won-der-ful gos-pel of Je - süs, Win-ning its way o'er the world;
Bringing the world from its bur - den Per-fect and blessed re - lease.
Now with the pow-ers of dark - ness E - ven the weakest may cope.
Wiping the tears from all fa - ces, Bidding all sor-row de - part.
I-dols, long rul-ing the na - tions, Soon from their thrones shall be hurled.
CHORUS.
Won-der-ful gos - pel! wonderful pow'r! Winning new vict'ries ev-e - ry hour;
Rul-ing the hearts of the children of men, Bidding them hope a - gain.

70. WILL YOU BE THERE?

ANON. D. E. DORTCH.

1. Be-yond this life of hope and fears, Be-yond this world of
2. Its glo-rious gates are closed to sin, Naught that de-files can
3. No droop-ing form, no tear-ful eye, No hea-vy head, no
4. Our Sav-iour once a mor-tal child—As mor-tal man by
5. Yes, I shall be in that fair land, And with the saints and
grief and tears, There is a re-gion fair; It knows no change and
en-ter in To mar its beau-ty rare; Up-on that bright e-
wea-ry sigh, No pain, no grief, no care; But joys which mor-tals
man re-viled, There ma-ny crowns doth wear; While thousand thousands
an-gels stand And all its glo-ries share. And there with Christ I'll
no decay—No night ob-scures its end-less day; Oh, say, will you be there?
ternal shore Earth's bitter curse is known no more; Oh, say, will you be there?
may not know, Like peaceful riv-ers ev-er flow! Oh, say, will you be there?
swell the strain Of glory to the Lamb once slain; Oh, say, will you be there?
ev-er stay;— In that e-ter-nal, hap-py day; Oh, say, will you be there?
REFRAIN.
Will you be there, will you be there? Oh, say, will you be there?
will you be there?
In that bright land of end-less day, Oh, say, will you be there?

71. FEARING NO DANGER.

E. D. MUND. E. S. LORENZ.

1. Fear-ing no - dan - ger, no an - gry foe, On-ward we go! On-ward we go! Fa - ces so bright-ly with cour - age glow,
2. Loud-ly the li - ons a-round may roar, On-ward we go! On-ward we go! Je - sus has bound them, they harm no more,
3. What tho' the gi - ants of sin op - pose, On-ward we go! On-ward we go! Pow - er di - vine on us God be - stows,
4. What tho' the bat - tle be fierce and long, On-ward we go! On-ward we go! Some day we'll join the tri - umphant throng,
On-ward we brave-ly go.
CHORUS.
Why should we fear? no ill can be-tide,
While Je - sus ev - er walks by our side! No harm we're
dread-ing, We're safe - ly tread-ing The way to end - less life.

72. WONDERFUL LOVE OF GOD.

MRS. D. M. HORNER. E. S. LORENZ.

1. Tell it abroad till the world shall hear, Won-der-ful love of God!
2. Fol - low-ing still how-so-e'er I stray, Won - der-ful love of God!
3. Bear-ing the shame of the cross for me, Won - der-ful love of God!
Free - ing my soul from its guilt and fear, Won - der-ful love of God!
Plant - ing the cross in my downward way, Won - der-ful love of God!
Nail - ing my sins to the cru - el tree, Won - der-ful love of God!
Bridging the chasm that so deep and wide Sever'd my soul from the Father's side;
Teaching by lessons of loss and pain, Earth and its pleasures are fleeting,-vain,
Help me to o - pen my heart's door wide, Let this great love of the Cru-ci-fied
Bid- ding me trust it whate'er be-tide, Won-der-ful love of God!
Christ and his grace can a - lone sus-tain, Won - der-ful love of God!
Sweep thro' my soul with resist - less tide, Won - der-ful love of God!
CHORUS.
Love! love! won - der - ful love! Join in its prais - es the -

WONDERFUL LOVE OF GOD. Concluded.

hosts a-bove! Love! love! love! Wonder-ful love of God!

73. DO IT NOW.

From "Glasgow Christian Leader."

D. E. DORTCH.

1. If you have a kind word, say it—Throbbing hearts soon sink to rest;
2. Can you do a kind deed, do it—From de-spair some soul to save;
3. If some great thing for to-mor-row You are dreaming, do it now;
4. Speak thy word, per-form thy du-ty—Night is com-ing with its rest;
FINE.
If you owe a kind-ness, pay it—Life's sun hur-ries to the west.
Bless each day as you pass thro' it, You are march-ing to the grave.
From the fu-ture do not bor-row; Frost soon gath-ers on the brow.
Stars will gleam in fade-less beau-ty, Grass-es whis-per o'er thy breast.
D. S.—If you mean to help an-oth-er, Do not wait but do it now.
CHORUS.
D. S.
Days for deeds are few, my broth-er, Then to-day ful-fill thy vow;

Controlled by D. E. Dortch.

74. **IT IS FINISHED.**

D. E. D. — D. E. DORTCH.

1. It is finished! cried the Saviour; man is ransomed from the fall, And the
2. It is finished! cried the Saviour, as he hung on Cal-va - ry; There is
3. It is finished! cried the Saviour, and he yielded up the ghost; He had
4. It is finished! cried the Saviour; there is rest for ev - 'ry soul, Who will
plan of his redemption is com-plete; It is finished! hal - le-lu - jah!
nothing more that an-y one can do; It is finished! hal - le-lu - jah!
made a way for men to be for-giv'n; It is finished! hal - le-lu - jah!
come and trust the Mighty One to save; It is finished! hal - le-lu - jah!
it is finished once for all, There is peace and pardon at the mer-cy seat.
his sal - va-tion now is free, And his grace is of-fered free-ly now to you.
shout the happy ransomed host, Who are walking in that blessed way to heav'n.
he can make the wounded whole; For the perishing his precious life he gave.
CHORUS.
It is finished! hal - le - lu - jah! it is finished! hal - le - lu - jah!
It is fin-ished, was the Sav-iour's dy - ing cry.
dy - ing cry.

Controlled by D. E. Dortch.

IT IS FINISHED. Concluded.

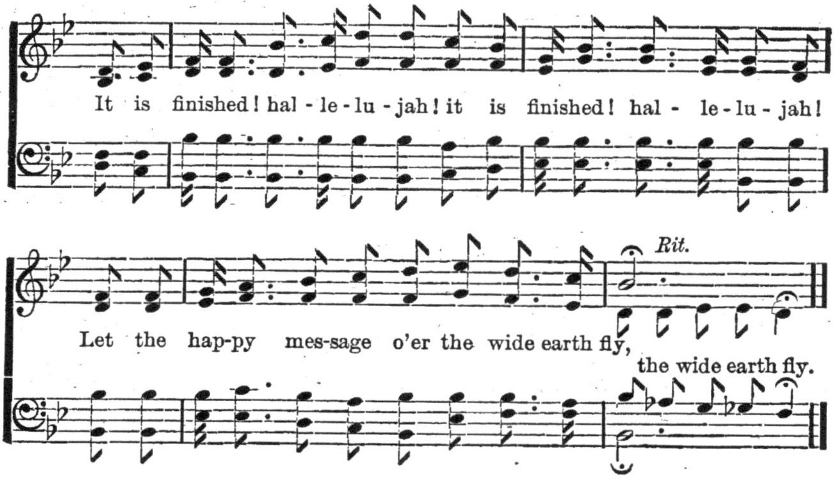
It is finished! hal - le - lu - jah! it is finished! hal - le - lu - jah!
Rit.
Let the hap-py mes-sage o'er the wide earth fly,
the wide earth fly.

75. A SOLDIER OF THE CROSS.

ANON. GEO. N. ALLEN.

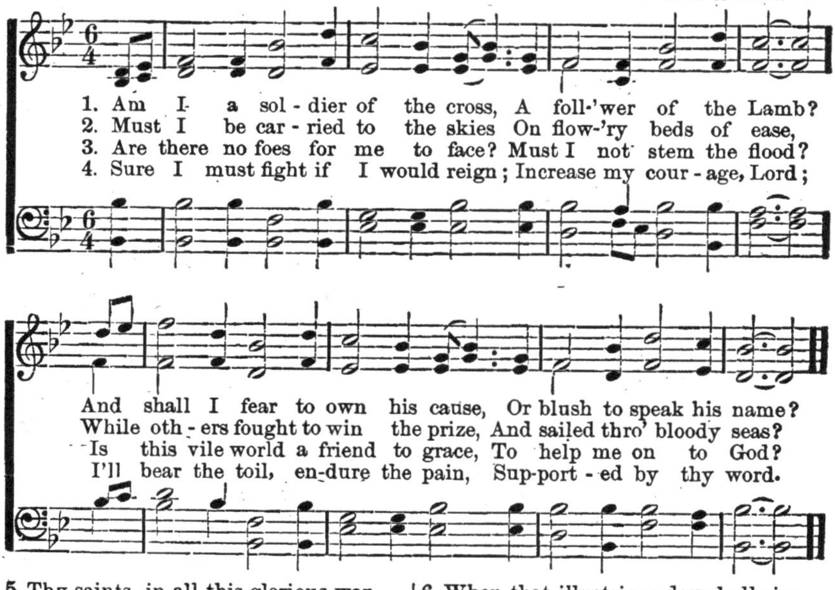
1. Am I a sol - dier of the cross, A foll-'wer of the Lamb?
2. Must I be car - ried to the skies On flow-'ry beds of ease,
3. Are there no foes for me to face? Must I not stem the flood?
4. Sure I must fight if I would reign; Increase my cour - age, Lord;
And shall I fear to own his cause, Or blush to speak his name?
While oth - ers fought to win the prize, And sailed thro' bloody seas?
Is this vile world a friend to grace, To help me on to God?
I'll bear the toil, en-dure the pain, Sup-port - ed by thy word.

5 Thy saints, in all this glorious war,
Shall conquer, though they die;
They see the triumph from afar,
By faith they bring it nigh.

6 When that illustrious day shall rise,
And all thy armies shine
In robes of vict'ry through the skies,
The glory shall be thine.

76. ALL FOR JESUS.

The last song composed and sung in public by its lamented author.
Written out from memory by a friend.

C. M. H. REV. C. M. HOTT.

1. All day long I'd bear the cross for Je - sus, He up - on it died for me; He from sin my bur-dened soul re - leas - es, And he gives me vic - to - ry.
2. All day long I'd glad - ly speak for Je - sus, He is plead - ing now for me; And his ten - der mer - cy nev - er ceas - es, Ev - er kind and true is he.
3. All day long I'd glad - ly work for Je - sus, Yield - ing him my ev - 'ry pow'r; Do - ing on - ly what the Mas - ter pleas - es, Ev - 'ry day and ev - 'ry hour.
4. All day long how sweet the love of Je - sus, Keep - ing, com - fort - ing my soul, While the light of glo - ry still in - creas - es, As the days shall o'er me roll.
CHORUS.
All day long I'd give him glo - ry, glo - ry, For he is so good to me;
All day long I'd tell the same sweet sto - ry, How he gave his life for me.

77. THERE IS MUSIC IN MY SOUL.

T. W. WILLIAMS. WILLIAM RUSSELL.

1. I was once in sin and far from God, And dis-cord reign'd su-preme;
2. Give me a heart that's tuned by God, A heart that's like his own;
3. All now I crave is that my heart May beat in time with Thine,
But now I'm sav'd thro' Je - sus' blood, My soul's tuned to that theme.
A heart that's wash'd in Je - sus' blood, A heart of pur - est tone.
Thy rich - est mel - o - dy im - part, And har - mo - ny di - vine.
CHORUS.
There is mu - sic in my soul, Sweet mu - sic in my soul, For
Christ has tuned my heart a - right; There is mu - sic in my soul,
Sweet mu - sic in my soul, For Christ has tuned my heart a - right.

78. SAIL ON.

PRISCILLA J. OWENS. E. S. LORENZ.

1. The waves roll high, the clouds are dark, Yet onward steers each Christian bark;
2. We will not fear the tempest's war, No shadow hides sweet Bethlehem's star;
3. With cheerful hearts we hold our way, The darkest night precedes the day,
Our homeward course we safe-ly keep, For Je-sus rules the wa-t'ry deep.
We trust in One, who guides and saves, We know that Jesus walks the waves.
This stormy blast will waft us o'er, Where Christ, our Lord, has gone before.
CHORUS.
Although the billows roar We shall reach the heav'nly shore; Sail on, ...
Sail on! sail on! sail on! sail on! Although the billows roar
sail on! Yes, al-though the bil-lows roar, We shall
We shall reach the heav'nly shore; Sail on! sail on! sail
reach the heav'nly shore; Sail on! . . . . sail on!
on! sail on! Yes, although the billows roar, We shall reach the heav'nly shore.
rit.

79. NEARING THE PORT.

REV. W. T. DALE. D. E. DORTCH.

1. I am nearing the port, I shall soon be at home, And the voy-age of life will be o'er; And beneath the high arch-es of heaven's bright dome, I shall dwell with my friends gone be-fore.
2. I am nearing the port, For the land is in sight, And the mountains e-ter-nal are seen; The bright land-scapes of E-den I hail with delight, And the plains that lie cov-ered with green.
3. I am nearing the port, I will soon be at rest, I will an-chor in peace by that strand; I will stand on the shore 'mid the throng of the blest, Those who dwell in that beau-ti-ful land.
4. I am nearing the port, See the bless-ed have come, They are gath'ring a-long on the shore; Now they watch to re-ceive me and welcome me home, There from them I will part nev-er-more.
5. When I've anchored in port, And have reach'd the bright strand, And the tempests of life all are past, With my Sav-iour I'll dwell in that beau-ti-ful land, While with rap-ture I'll shout, "Home at last!"
D. S.—Then I'll hear the sweet voic-es of lov'd ones now there, On the beau-ti-ful, glit-ter-ing shore.
FINE.
CHORUS.
I am near-ing . . .
I am nearing the port,
Yes near-ing the port, Soon the voy-age of life will be o'er;
D.S.

Controlled by D. E. Dortch.

6. Round Notes.

80. COME TO THE WATERS.

E. R. LATTA. E. S. LORENZ.

1. Come to the wa-ters of life! Sin-ner a-thirst, draw nigh!
2. Come to the wa-ters of life! Wa-ters that God doth give!
3. Come to the wa-ters of life! Free-ly for all they flow!
Out in the des-ert of sin, Why will you thirsting die?
Wa-ters that nev-er shall fail, Long as the soul shall live!
Je-sus in-vites you to come, Je-sus who loves you so!
Long you have wander'd from God! Far you have gone a-stray!
Sin has your spir-it un-done! You are of sin the slave!
Do not re-fuse him, and die! Drink of the heal-ing tide!
But there is mer-cy for you, If you re-turn to-day!
Je-sus has suf-fered for you! Je-sus a-lone can save!
Come to the wa-ters of life! Drink and be sat-is-fied!
CHORUS.
Come! come! come to the wa-ters, O
Come to the wa-ters, O come! Come,

COME TO THE WATERS. Concluded.

souls that for wa - ter brooks pant; Come! Come!
drink, drink, drink ye and live, Come to the wa-ters, O

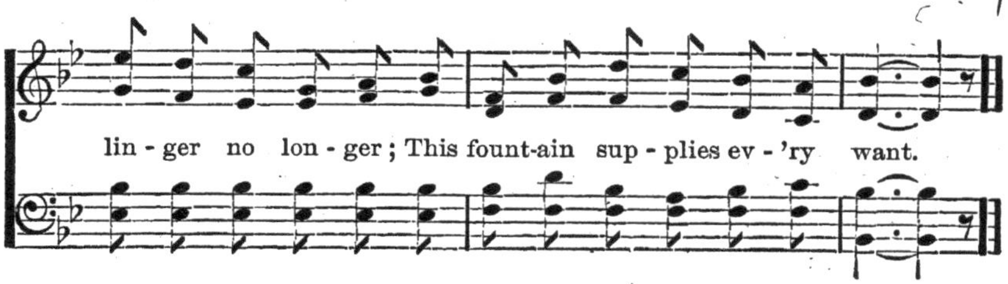
lin - ger no lon - ger; This fount-ain sup - plies ev - 'ry want.

81. NEW HAVEN.

RAY PALMER. THOS. HASTINGS.

1. My faith looks up to thee, Thou Lamb of Cal-va-ry; Saviour di-vine; Now hear me
2. May thy rich grace impart Strength to my fainting heart, My zeal in-spire; As thou hast
3. While life's dark maze I tread, And griefs around me spread, Be thou my Guide; Bid dark-ness
4. When ends life's transient dream, When death's cold, sullen stream Shall o'er me roll, Blest Saviour!

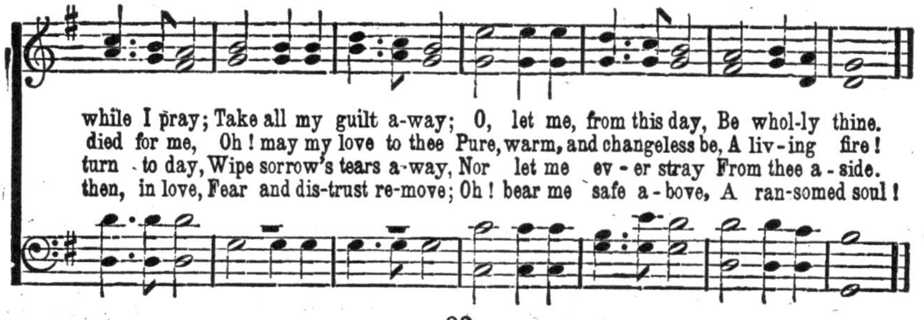
while I pray; Take all my guilt a-way; O, let me, from this day, Be whol-ly thine.
died for me, Oh! may my love to thee Pure, warm, and changeless be, A liv-ing fire!
turn to day, Wipe sorrow's tears a-way, Nor let me ev - er stray From thee a - side.
then, in love, Fear and dis-trust re-move; Oh! bear me safe a-bove, A ran-somed soul!

82. THERE'S A LIGHT AT THE RIVER.

ARR. FROM D. M. CASEY. D. E. DORTCH.

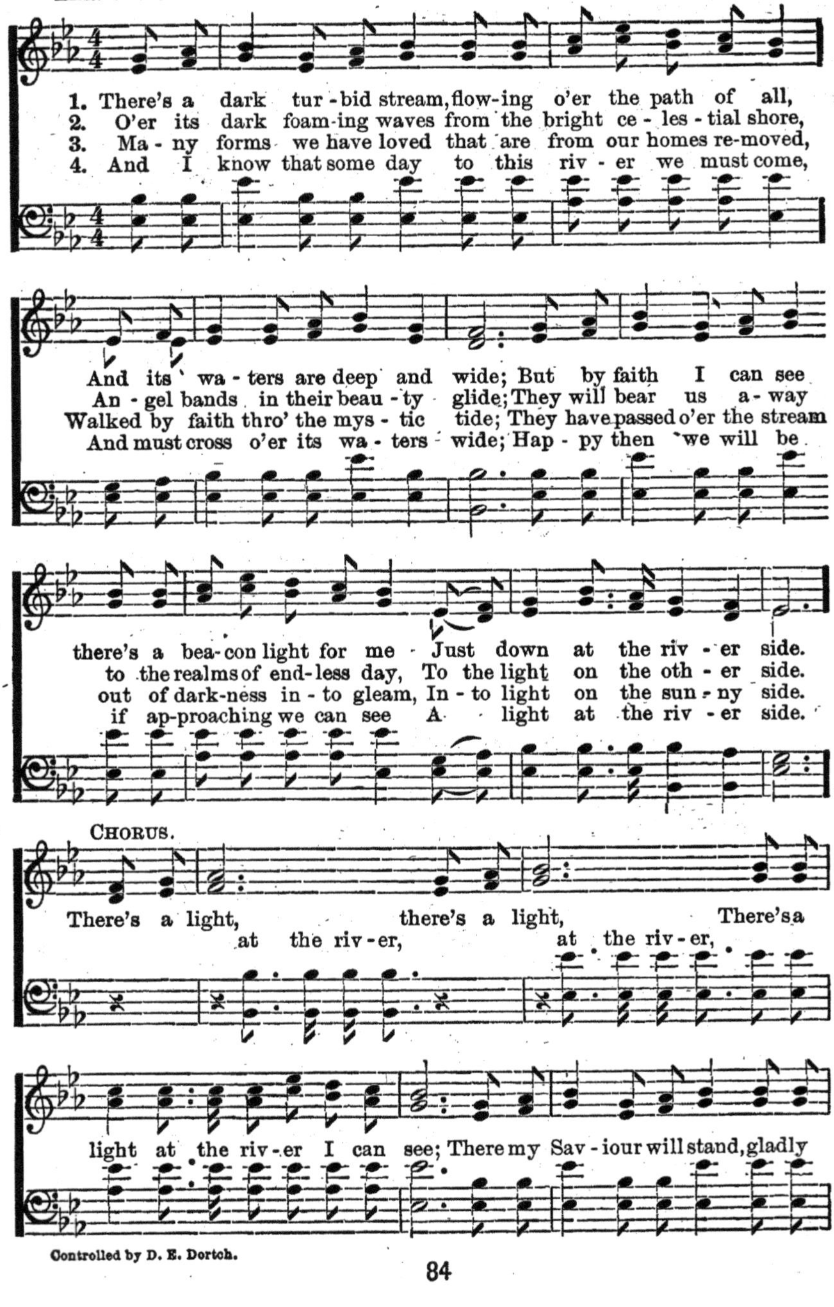
1. There's a dark tur-bid stream, flow-ing o'er the path of all,
2. O'er its dark foam-ing waves from the bright ce-les-tial shore,
3. Ma-ny forms we have loved that are from our homes re-moved,
4. And I know that some day to this riv-er we must come,
And its wa-ters are deep and wide; But by faith I can see
An-gel bands in their beau-ty glide; They will bear us a-way
Walked by faith thro' the mys-tic tide; They have passed o'er the stream
And must cross o'er its wa-ters wide; Hap-py then we will be
there's a bea-con light for me Just down at the riv-er side.
to the realms of end-less day, To the light on the oth-er side.
out of dark-ness in-to gleam, In-to light on the sun-ny side.
if ap-proaching we can see A light at the riv-er side.
CHORUS.
There's a light, there's a light, There's a
at the riv-er, at the riv-er,
light at the riv-er I can see; There my Sav-iour will stand, gladly

THERE'S A LIGHT AT THE RIVER. Concluded.

hold-ing in his hand A light at the riv-er for me,
for me.

83. REDEEMING LOVE.

J. A. C. ARR. JOHN TIBBALLS.

1. Redeeming Love! Redeeming love! This is the theme of saints a-bove;
2. The an-gel hosts all wond'ring see, But fail to solve the mys-ter-y;
3. 'Tis here on earth the pow'r is giv'n To sing the sweet-est song of heav'n;
4. Oh, shout a-loud, ye sons of men! Tell the glad tid-ings o'er a-gain;

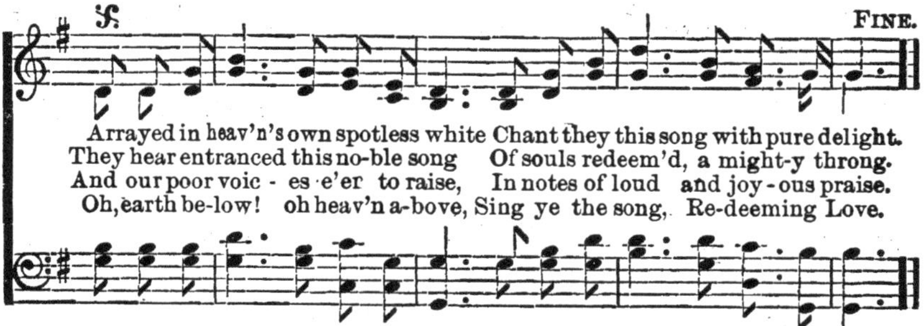
FINE.
Arrayed in heav'n's own spotless white Chant they this song with pure delight.
They hear entranced this no-ble song Of souls redeem'd, a might-y throng.
And our poor voic-es e'er to raise, In notes of loud and joy-ous praise.
Oh, earth be-low! oh heav'n a-bove, Sing ye the song, Re-deeming Love.

D. S.—*Redeem-ing love! Redeeming love! We join the song, Re-deem-ing love.*

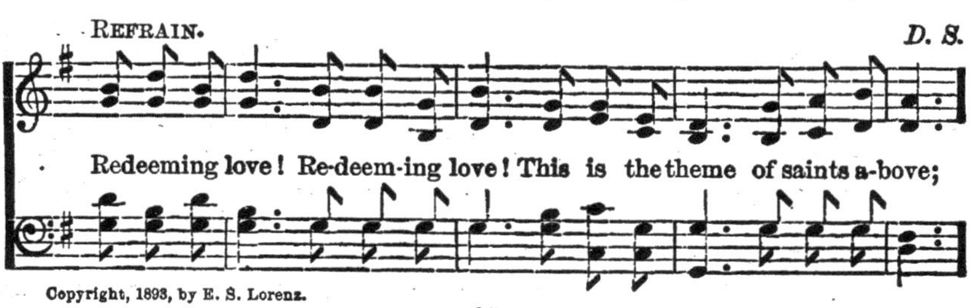
REFRAIN.
D. S.
Redeeming love! Re-deem-ing love! This is the theme of saints a-bove;

84. CHRIST ASSURES US.

REV. GEO. P. HOTT. JAS. H. RUEBUSH.

1. No one hath told me what this life shall be, If full of sor - row, or
2. No one hath told me where this life will end, Whether with stranger, or
3. No one hath told me what these eyes shall see, When I a-wake in e -
joy for me; But Christ assures us no ill can be - fall Those who on
con-stant friend; But Christ assures us, from whatever clime, Sin-ners re -
ter - ni - ty; But Christ assures us that hope's still in store, "He that be -
Je - sus for help ev-er call.
turn-ing "shall ev-er be mine."
liev - eth" shall live ev-er - more.
CHORUS.
Blessed as - sur - ance, lov-ing en -
dur-ance, Christ is our friend, yes, "world without end"; Blessed as -
sur - ance, lov-ing endurance, "World without end," yes, Christ is our friend.

85. SALVATION IS FREE.

JOHN McPHERSON. CHAS. EDW. POLLOCK.

1. Sal - va - tion is free for you and for me, The fountain is opened on Cal - va-ry's side; There Jesus bought peace from sin full re-lease; For poor dy-ing sin-ners he died.
2. Sal - va - tion for all! now on his name call, And bow and con-fess at the dear Saviour's feet; On him cast your care each burden he'll bear, And grant you a par-don complete.
3. Sal - va - tion at last when earth life is past, He'll grant you when ent-'ring the heav-en-ly door; In that home of light so glorious and bright, We'll meet there to part nevermore.
Rit.
CHORUS.
Sal - va - tion is free, to Je - sus now flee, O sin-ner no lon-ger de-lay; Now fall at his feet, ac-cept par-don sweet, The Sav-iour is call-ing to-day.
Rit.

Controlled by D. E. Dortch.

86. WHAT MUST I DO TO BE SAVED?

D. E. DORTCH. D. E. DORTCH.

saved?"
re - ly,
1. "Sirs, what must I do to be, do to be sav'd?" Was the jailor's earn - est
2. Oh, what must I do to be, do to be sav'd?" For my sins o'erwhelm me
3. Oh, what must I do to be, do to be sav'd?" Is there par-don at the
4. If you will on Je-sus, on Je-sus re - ly, He will make you white as
plea; He felt his great need of sal - va - tion, For he was as
so; My heart is now breaking with - in me, Oh, where for re -
cross? Will Je - sus, the Sav - iour for sin - ners, Re-ceive me and
snow; Oh, plead then for mer - cy and par-don, He'll cleanse and for-
Chorus.
saved?
vile as could be.
lief can I go?
save me from loss?
give you, I know.
Oh, what must I do to be, do to be saved?
saved?
Oh, what must I do to be, do to be saved? My sins are ma-ny, my
rit.
sor - rows sore, Oh, what must I do to be sav'd, to be saved?

87. PRAISE.

H. F. JAMES. E. S. LORENZ.

1. Praise to the Fa-ther; great is he and glo-rious, Guid-ing the
2. Praise to the Sav-iour, full of grace and glo-ry, Leav-ing his
3. Praise to the Spir-it, in our hearts a-bid-ing, Fill-ing with
stars of light with e-qual hand; Bring him your prais-es,
throne, on earth to live and die; Earth, join your voi-ces,
light where dark-ness once had reigned; Grate-ful-ly praise him,
louder swell the cho-rus, Bow ye a-dor-ing, sons of ev-'ry land.
tell the wondrous sto-ry, Ev-er ex-alt his name who rules on high.
comforting and guid-ing, Giv-ing as-surance of sal-va-tion gained.
CHORUS.
Praise to the Fa-ther, great is he and glo-rious,
Praise to the Son, o'er sin and death vic-to-rious,
Praise to the Spir-it, loud-er swell the cho-rus, Praise ye the Lord.

88. THERE IS NO FRIEND LIKE JESUS.

R. H. LYON. D. E. DORTCH.

1. There is a Friend, a Friend in need, A Friend with God to in - ter-cede,
2. A Friend to guide thee day by day, And by thy side to guard the way,
3. What matchless love was this for thee! From heav'n above to earth's de-gree,
4. Yield to him now, no more de-lay, Thy spir - it bow, his voice o - bey—
His pre - cious name is Je - sus; A Friend thy soul to save from sin,
A lov - ing Friend is Je - sus; A Friend whose pow'r a-lone can cheer
He came, the pre-cious Je - sus; He bled and died thy soul to save,
Ac-cept this pre-cious Je - sus; Oh, then to thee, thy sins forgiv'n,
And make thee whole and pure with-in, Oh, such a Friend is Je - sus!
In that dark hour when death is near—No earth - ly Friend like Je - sus!
For thee con-quer'd death and grave, Oh, what a Friend is Je - sus!
Thy joy will be, in earth and heav'n, For-ev - er-more with Je - sus.
CHORUS.
'Tis Je - sus, bless - ed Je - sus, There is no Friend like Je - sus;
'Tis Je - sus, bless - ed Je - sus, There is no friend like Je-sus.

Controlled by D. E. Dortch.

89. HAIL YE THE KING.

ANNA CHICHESTER. E. S. LORENZ.

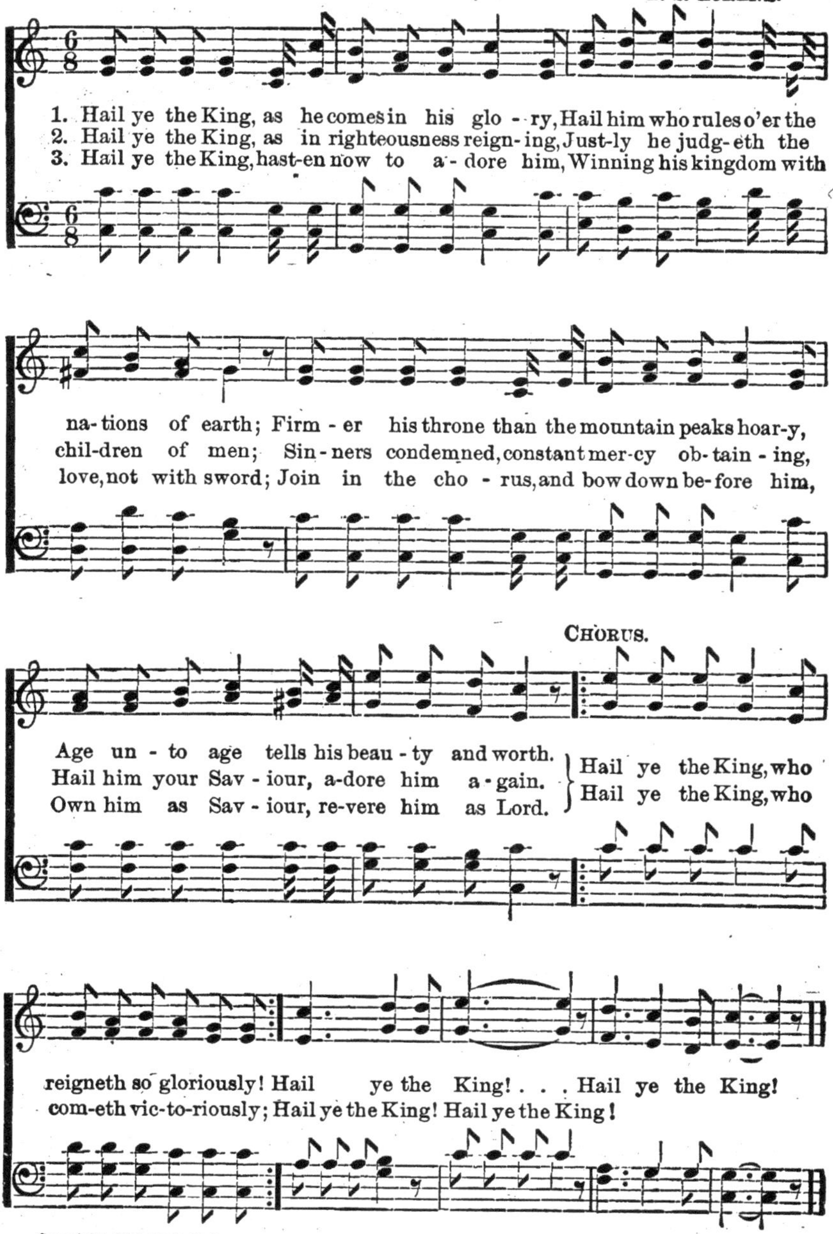
1. Hail ye the King, as he comes in his glo - - ry, Hail him who rules o'er the
2. Hail ye the King, as in righteousness reign-ing, Just-ly he judg-eth the
3. Hail ye the King, hast-en now to a - dore him, Winning his kingdom with
na-tions of earth; Firm - er his throne than the mountain peaks hoar-y,
chil-dren of men; Sin-ners condemned, constant mer-cy ob-tain - ing,
love, not with sword; Join in the cho - rus, and bow down be-fore him,
Age un - to age tells his beau - ty and worth.
Hail him your Sav - iour, a-dore him a - gain.
Own him as Sav - iour, re-vere him as Lord.
CHORUS.
Hail ye the King, who
Hail ye the King, who
reigneth so gloriously! Hail ye the King! . . . Hail ye the King!
com-eth vic-to-riously; Hail ye the King! Hail ye the King!

90. THE DAY OF DAYS.

E. D. MUND. E. S. LORENZ.

1. Fill with loft - y praise This the day of days, Whose ef - ful- gent rays
2. God him-self draws near, Greets his children here, Bring-ing life and cheer
3. Souls released, take wing! Rise from earth, and sing Praises to your King,
Fill all the world with light; In its beau - ty drest,
To those who love his name; Gives from care re- lease,
And spread his fame a - broad; When our Sab - baths end,
Let the world, at rest, Find- ing vig - or blest, In God's dear praise u - nite.
For our tri - als peace; Bids our doubtings cease; Asks us his grace to claim.
Sab-bath we shall spend Where our praise shall blend With choirs who praise our God.
CHORUS.
Day of days! . . . we hail thy coming fair and sweet! Joy and praise . .
Day of days! Joy and praise
a-lone for thy blest hours are meet! All thy moments God has blest, Promise

sweet of fu - ture rest, And our lives thou makest ful - ler, more complete.

91. HOW I LOVE JESUS.

FREDERICK WHITFIELD. AMERICAN SPIRITUAL.

1. There is a name I love to hear, I love to sing its worth;
2. It tells me of a Saviour's love, Who died to set - me free;
3. It tells me what my Fa - ther hath In store for ev - 'ry day,
4. It tells of One whose lov - ing heart Can feel my deepest woe,
It sounds like mu - sic in mine ear, The sweetest name on earth.
It tells me of his pre - cious blood, The sin - ner's per - fect plea.
And, though I tread a dark - some path, Yields sunshine all the way.
Who in each sor - row bears a part, That none can bear be - low.
CHORUS.
Oh, how I love Je - sus, Oh, how I love Je - sus,
Oh, how I love Je - sus, Be - cause he first loved me.

92. IT REDEEMED ME.

D. E. D. D. E. DORTCH.

1. I was once in sin and the dark-ness of the night, But the precious Saviour's blood redeemed me; I was vile with-in, could not see a ray of light, But the precious Saviour's blood redeemed me.
2. I was bowed with grief, and my guilt op-pressed me sore, But the precious Saviour's blood redeemed me; Je-sus gave re-lief and in sin I walk no more, For the precious Saviour's blood redeemed me.
3. When in faith I came I could feel the cleans-ing power, Then the precious Saviour's blood redeemed me; Now I praise his name and will praise him ev-'ry hour, For the precious Saviour's blood redeemed me.
4. Soon my soul shall fly to that ci-ty of pure gold, For the precious Saviour's blood redeemed me; In that home on high his own face I shall be-hold, For the precious Saviour's blood redeemed me.
CHORUS.
It re-deemed me, it re-deemed me,
It redeemed, redeemed, it redeemed, redeemed, 'Twas the precious Saviour's

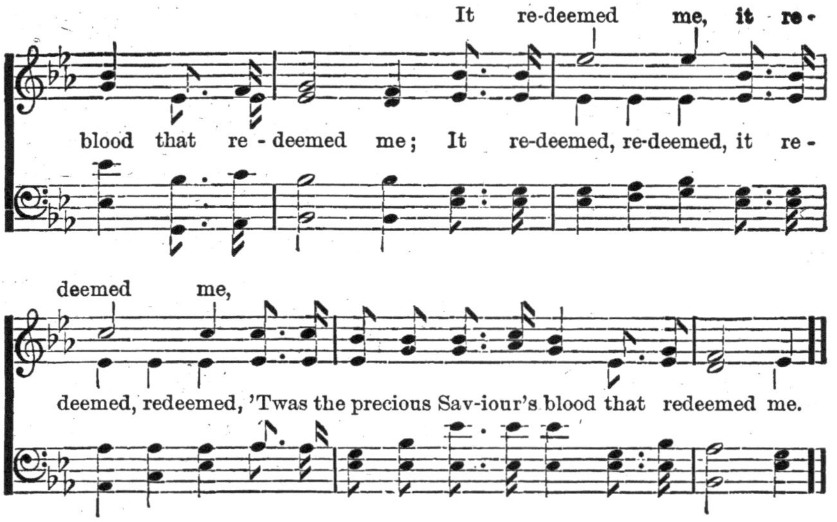
It re-deemed me, it re-
blood that re - deemed me; It re-deemed, re-deemed, it re-
deemed me,
deemed, redeemed, 'Twas the precious Sav-iour's blood that redeemed me.

93. LORD, I HAVE MADE THY WORD MY CHOICE.

ISAAC WATTS. W. H. HAVERGAL.

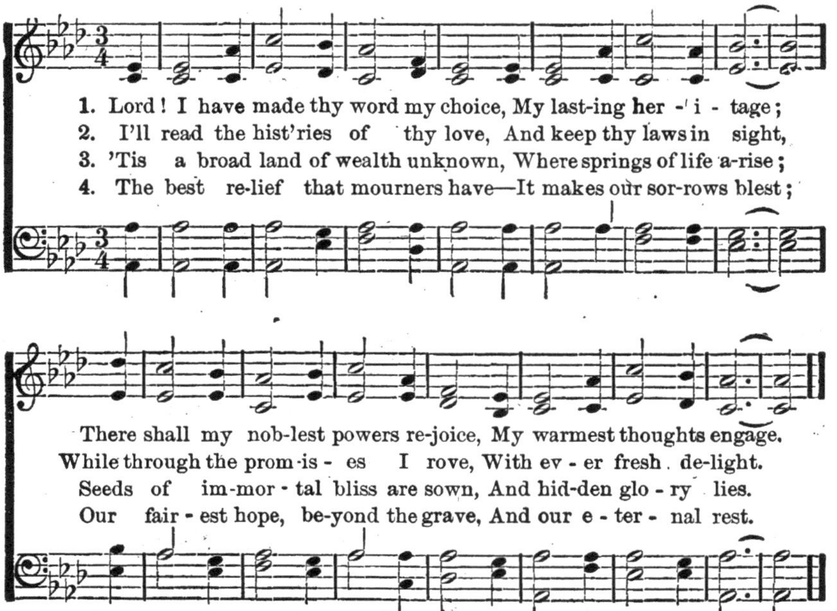
1. Lord! I have made thy word my choice, My last-ing her - i - tage;
2. I'll read the hist'ries of thy love, And keep thy laws in sight,
3. 'Tis a broad land of wealth unknown, Where springs of life a-rise;
4. The best re-lief that mourners have—It makes our sor-rows blest;
There shall my nob-lest powers re-joice, My warmest thoughts engage.
While through the prom-is - es I rove, With ev - er fresh de-light.
Seeds of im-mor - tal bliss are sown, And hid-den glo - ry lies.
Our fair - est hope, be-yond the grave, And our e - ter - nal rest.

94. ARE YOU READY FOR SERVICE?

JESSIE H. BROWN. E. S. LORENZ.

1. Should the "Forward march!" be echoed down the lines to-day, Would it find you fac-ing tow'rd the foe? Is your ar-mor buckled tight-ly? Are your weapons burnished brightly? Are you ready, should the call be, "Go?"
2. Should the bu-gle-note of bat-tle come to you to-day, Would the summons find you nerv'd for fight? Are your pul-ses true and steady? Could you an-swer, "I am ready!" If the foe were marshalled just in sight?"
3. Should the call to death and judgment reach your ear to-day, Would it find you in the bat-tling host? At the ev-en or the morning, Should it come without a warning, Would the mes-sage find you at your post?
D. S.—read-y for his ser-vice?
FINE.
Are you read-y for his ser-vice? Will you dare to be a sol-dier true!
CHORUS.
Are you read-y for the ser-vice of Je-ho-vah?
are you read-y for it now?
Hear his summons ring-ing out to you, (out to you:) Are you
D.S.

95. THE MASTER WELCOMES THE CHILDREN.

JENNIE WILSON. D. E. DORTCH.

DUET.
1. A beau - ti - ful sto - ry in God's book is told Of Je - sus so
2. His hands in kind blessing on chil-dren were laid When earth was our
3. The lov - ing Lord welcomes the lit - tle ones still As fond - ly as
4. Oh, go for the glo - ri - fied Mas-ter's dear sake, His gen - tle com -
pure and mild; As ea - ger throngs gathered around him of old He
Saviour's home; "Of such is the king-dom of heaven," he said, And
he did then; To bring them to Je - sus is do - ing his will, He
mand re - peat; The hands of the lit - tle ones lov-ing - ly take, And
CHORUS.
welcom'd the humblest child.
ten - der - ly bade them come.
calls them to him a - gain.
lead them to Je - sus' feet.
The Mas-ter still welcomes the chil-dren,
Lead them to him, yes, lead them to him; If ye love him go
out in the highway of life, And guide lit - tle feet to the Sav-iour.

7. Round Notes.

96. HOSANNA IN THE HIGHEST.

FOR THE SCHOOL.

REV. C. R. BLACKALL. E. S. LORENZ.

1. O Zi-on re-joice for thy King, Who cometh with tidings of peace,
2. He com-eth to break the strong bands That sin hath made heavy and sore;
3. Sing praise to the King o-ver all, Who com-eth to claim but his own,
And hast-en thy trib-ute to bring, To him whose reign never shall cease!
O cap-tives, be-fore you he stands, And sin hath do-min-ion no more:
In wor-ship let an-gels e'en fall, For mer-cy and love he hath shown;
DUET.
Mes-si-ah comes near, No more shalt thou fear, For the Day-spring from
A Sav-iour will he For ev-er-more be, Our Emman-u-el
Lift high the glad song, The notes full pro-long, The Re-dem-er our
heav-en shines clear; Mes-si-ah comes near, No more shalt thou fear,
all shall a-dore! A Sav-iour will he For ev-er-more be,
sin will a-tone! Lift high the glad song, The notes full pro-long,
For the Day-spring from heaven shines clear.
Our Em-man-u-el all shall a-dore.
The Re-deem-er our sins will a-tone.
CHORUS.
Ho-san-na! Ho-
Sing ho-san-na!

HOSANNA IN THE HIGHEST. Concluded.

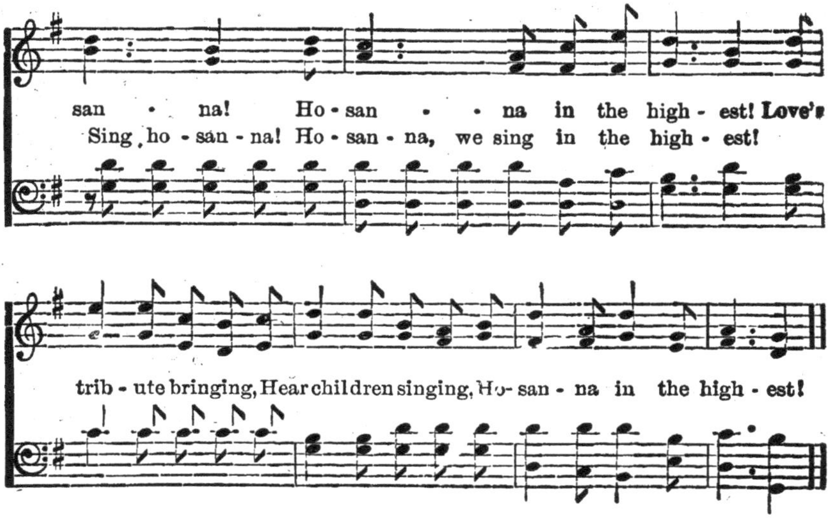
san - na! Ho - san - - na in the high - est! Love's
Sing, ho - san - na! Ho - san - na, we sing in the high - est!
trib - ute bringing, Hear children singing, Ho- san - na in the high - est!

97 I'LL LIVE FOR HIM.

C. R. DUNBAR.

1. My life, my love I give to thee, Thou Lamb of God, who died for me;
2. I now be-lieve thou dost re-ceive, For thou hast died that I might live;
3. Oh, thou who died on Cal - va- ry, To save my soul and make me free,
CHO.—I'll live for him who died for me, How hap- py then my life shall be!
D.C.
Oh, may I ev - er faith - ful be, My Sav- iour and my God.
And now henceforth I'll trust in thee, My Sav- iour and my God.
I con - se-crate my life to thee, My Sav- iour and my God.
I'll live for him who died for me, My Sav- iour and my God.

By per. of author

98. CAST YOUR BREAD.

E. B. LATTA. E. S. LORENZ.

1. Cast your bread . . up-on the wa-ters! Let them bear it where they may!
2. Cast your bread . . up-on the wa-ters, In the burn-ing noontide ray!
3. Cast your bread . . up-on the wa-ters! Feed the hun-gry! clothe the cold!
Not in vain, . . shall it be scat-tered You shall gath-er it some day!
Cast it in . . . the ros-y ev-'ning! Cast it in the morning gray!
Tell the sto - ry of redemp-tion, To the young and to the old!
When or how, you need not ques-tion! Trust the prom-ise you have read!
God will bless it! he has promised! He will keep his word with you!
Soon or late, 'twill glad your spir-it! It will be as God has said!
You have but . . . to do your du-ty! You have but to cast your bread!
Do then just . . what he has bid-den, That is all you have to do!
You shall gath - er, surely gath-er, If you on - ly cast your bread!
CHORUS.
Cast your bread upon the waters! Cast your bread up-on the waters!
Cast your bread upon the waters wide; Send it forth to bless on ev'ry tide;

CAST YOUR BREAD. Concluded.

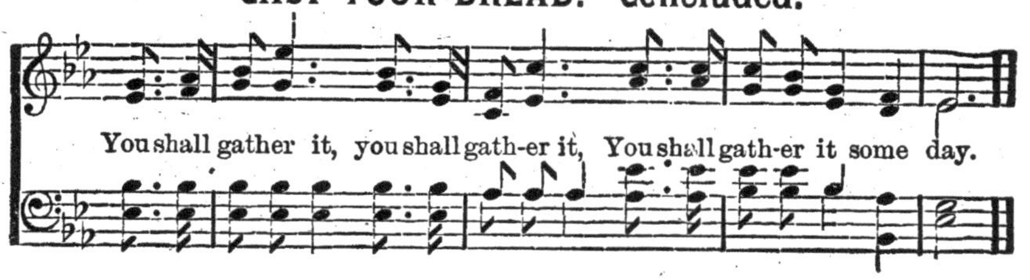
You shall gather it, you shall gath-er it, You shall gath-er it some day.

99. GOD SPEED THEM ON.

(Missionary Song.)

MRS. C. L. SHADDOCK. E. HANKS.

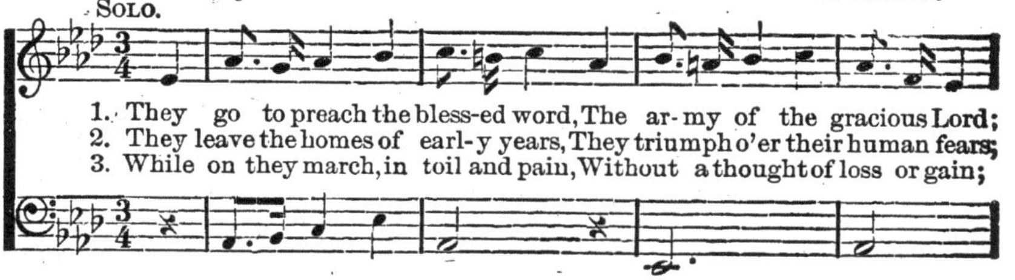
Solo.
1. They go to preach the bless-ed word, The ar-my of the gracious Lord;
2. They leave the homes of earl-y years, They triumph o'er their human fears;
3. While on they march, in toil and pain, Without a thought of loss or gain;

A-gainst the host of death and sin, A war to wage, a vic-t'ry won.
As sol-diers of the cross they bear His roy-al ban-ner ev-ery-where.
In ar-mor clad to meet the foe, God speed them on the way they go.

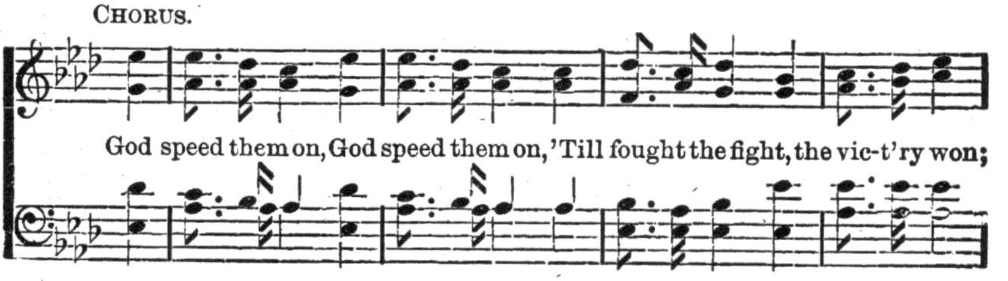
Chorus.
God speed them on, God speed them on, 'Till fought the fight, the vic-t'ry won;

'Till truth shall spread from shore to shore, 'Till death and sin shall be no more.

Controlled by D. E. Dortch

100. HOSANNA TO JESUS.

JENNIE WILSON. J. R. VALENTINE.

1. Ho-san-na to Je-sus, the loving friend of children; The guide who goes be-
2. Ho-san-na to Je-sus, the ev-er faith-ful shepherd, Who longs each lamb to
3. Ho-san-na to Je-sus, the wise, unerr-ing teach-er; The laws of God's pure
4. Ho-san-na to Je-sus, our blessed Lord and Saviour, Who gave his life a
fore us, ev-er true and kind, To mark for us safe pathways where our
shel-ter safe-ly in his fold, To guard them from all e-vil in his
kingdom we of him may learn; When hard seem life's stern lessons he is
ran-som that our souls might live. To him praise and glo-ry be thro' e-
eag-er foot-steps In fol-low-ing his lead-ing shall no dan-ger find.
ten-der keep-ing And lead them to the cit-y of un-tar-nished gold.
ev-er will-ing To help us in our weakness if to him we turn.
ter-nal a-ges, Let all the world to Je-sus grateful hom-age give.
CHORUS.
Ho-san-na to Je-sus, the ho-ly Son of Da-vid; As sang the
Jew-ish children, so we glad-ly sing: Ho-san-na to Je-sus, ho-

rit.
san-na in the highest, Let hap-py youthful voices with his prais-es ring.

101. GROWING IN GRACE.

E. D. MUND. E. S. LORENZ.

1. Help me, Sav-iour, more each day, Glad-ly thy sweet will o-bey;
2. Pur-er, ho-lier I would be, From my sin com-plete-ly free;
3. Out of dawn-ing in-to light, Out of grop-ing in-to sight,
4. Press-ing on to win the prize, Crown and throne be-fore my eyes,
FINE.
More and more thy love dis-play, Oh, help me grow in grace!
Draw me, Sav-iour, near-er thee, And help me grow in grace.
Out of weak-ness in-to might, Oh, help me grow in grace!
Let my soul's am-bi-tion rise, And help me grow in grace.
D. S.—Help me, Sav-iour, thou hast pow'r, To ev-er grow in grace.
CHORUS.
D.S.
Grow-ing in grace ev-'ry day, Grow-ing in grace ev-'ry hour,

102. PEACE, BE STILL.

(Male Quartet.)

D. M. JAMES. CHAS. H. GABRIEL.

1. When our hearts are sad and wea - ry, When our paths seem lone and
2. Do we grieve at man's be-hav - ior? Mourn we all in vain our
3. Have you heard his voice within you? Does the joy it brings con-
drear - y, Sweet the voice can make us cheer - y, Peace, be still.
la - bor, Pre-cious ac - cents of our Sav - iour, Peace, be still.
tin - ue? From all e - vil may it win you, Peace, be still.
When we meet with trib - u - la - tion, Chaf-ing un - der sore temp-
Can the Lord for - get us ev - er? Can his love from us e'er
Soon will drop our heav - y cross - es, Re-compensed for all our
ta - tion, Bless the Lord for con - so - la - tion, Peace, be still.
sev - er? Ours may fail but his, ah, nev - er! Peace, be still.
loss - es, An-chored safe where storm ne'er toss - es, Peace, be still.
CHORUS.
In all thy ways, ... Oh, seek his guid - ing, . . .
In all thy ways, Oh, seek his guiding; 'Mid all

PEACE, BE STILL. Concluded.

A-mid all troubles still confid-ing, In his grace . . . and
troub - - les still con-fid - ing . . . In his grace
ritard e dim.
pow'r a - bid - ing, . . . Peace, be still, peace, be still. . . . . .
and pow'r abid-ing, Peace, be still, peace, be still.

103. SITTING AT THE FEET OF JESUS.

PRISCILLA J. OWENS. E. S. LORENZ.

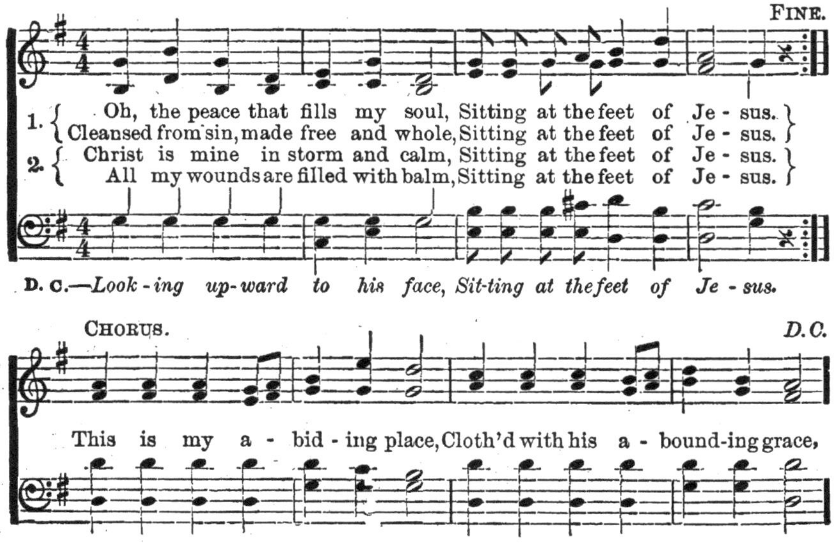
FINE.
1. { Oh, the peace that fills my soul, Sitting at the feet of Je - sus.
Cleansed from sin, made free and whole, Sitting at the feet of Je - sus. }
2. { Christ is mine in storm and calm, Sitting at the feet of Je - sus.
All my wounds are filled with balm, Sitting at the feet of Je - sus. }
D. C.—Look - ing up-ward to his face, Sit-ting at the feet of Je - sus.
CHORUS. D.C.
This is my a - bid - ing place, Cloth'd with his a - bound-ing grace,

3 Here I rest from toil and strife,
Sitting at the feet of Jesus;
Safe beneath the Tree of Life,
Sitting at the feet of Jesus.

4 Come ye guilty and be healed,
Sitting at the feet of Jesus;
Freely in God's love revealed,
Sitting at the feet of Jesus.

104. WHERE HE LEADS I'LL FOLLOW.

W. A. O. W. A. OGDEN.

1. Sweet are the prom-is - es, Kind is the word; Dear-er far than
2. Sweet is the ten-der love Je - sus hath shown; Sweeter far than
3. List to his lov-ing words, "Come un - to me"; Wea-ry, heav-y
an - y mes-sage man ev - er heard. Pure was the mind of Christ,
an - y love that mor - tals have known. Kind to the er - ring one,
la - den, there is sweet rest for thee; Trust in his prom-is - es,
Sin - less I see; He the great ex - am - ple is and
Faith - ful is he; He the great ex - am - ple is and
Faith - ful and sure; Lean up - on the Sav - iour, and thy
pat - tern for me.
pat - tern for me.
soul is se - cure.
CHORUS.
Where . . . . he leads I'll
Where he leads I'll fol - low,
fol - - - low, Fol - - low all the
where he leads I'll fol - low, fol-low all the way, yes,

WHERE HE LEADS I'LL FOLLOW. Concluded.

way, Where . . . . . . he leads I'll
fol - low all the way, Where he leads I'll fol - low,
fol - - - - low, Fol-low Je-sus ev - 'ry day.
Where he leads I'll fol - low,

105. SOFTLY FADES THE TWILIGHT RAY.

SAMUEL F. SMITH. L. M. GOTTSCHALK.

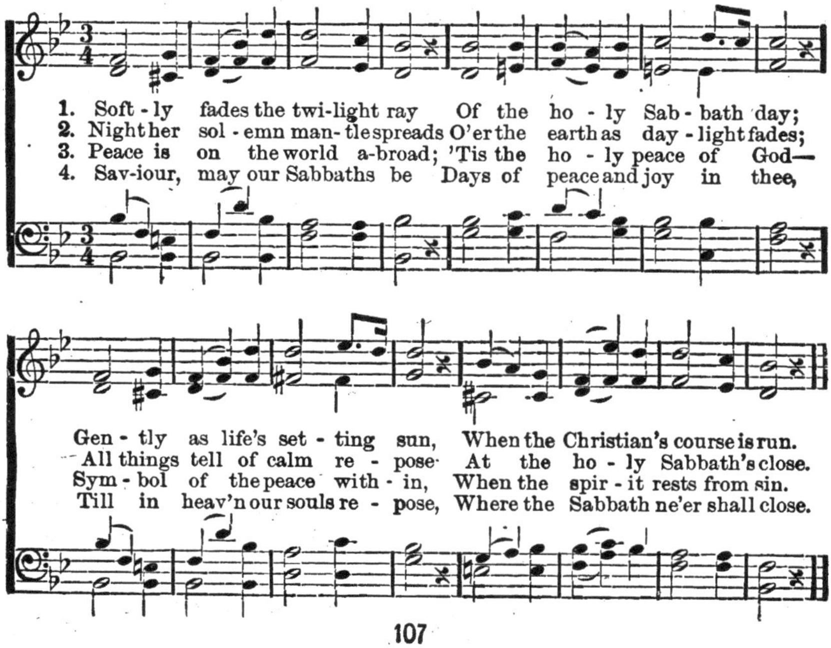
1. Soft - ly fades the twi-light ray Of the ho - ly Sab - bath day;
2. Night her sol - emn man - tle spreads O'er the earth as day - light fades;
3. Peace is on the world a-broad; 'Tis the ho - ly peace of God—
4. Sav-iour, may our Sabbaths be Days of peace and joy in thee,
Gen - tly as life's set - ting sun, When the Christian's course is run.
All things tell of calm re - pose At the ho - ly Sabbath's close.
Sym - bol of the peace with - in, When the spir - it rests from sin.
Till in heav'n our souls re - pose, Where the Sabbath ne'er shall close.

106. GO YE INTO ALL THE WORLD.

Dedicated to Chaplain McCabe.

WM. M. DARWOOD, D. D. REV. R. L. SELLE.

1. Ye mes-sen-gers of grace, ye flaming heralds, go To ev-'ry clime and
2. My gos-pel's one of grace; to all mankind 'tis given; It seeks to save the
3. Lord, we o - bey thy call, we'll to the nations go; And tell them of the
4. Ring out the blessed sound, praise to our God be given, And Jesus Christ his
coast, and let the na-tions know My gos-pel's one of light to those in
race, and lift it up to heav'n. My gos-pel's one of power to those that
blood that wash-es white as snow; On Congo's mighty stream, on Tan-gan-
Son, who brought us home to heav'n; Sal-va-tion to the Lamb, the Lamb for
darkness chain'd, To those in black-est night, where sin so long has reigned.
shall be-lieve; E'en those who murder'd me, the mes-sage may re - ceive.
i - ka's shore, We'll spread the glorious truth that man may sin no more.
sin-ners slain, Ring out, the work is done: reign, Christ, for-ev-er reign.
CHORUS.
Go in - to all the world, To all the na - tions go;
And tell them of the blood that wash - es white as snow.

From "Choicest Gems," by per R. L. Selle, Fort Worth, Tex.

107. THE WONDROUS NAME.

MARK ADAMS. REV. A. A. ARMEN.

1. We have heard a name of pow - er, All the na-tions it shall thrill;
2. We have heard a name of glad-ness, Earth bowed down is filled with joy;
3. We have heard a name of glo - ry, Earth its full - ness can-not reach;
It shall men with new life dow-er, Stubborn hearts subdue and fill.
Songs of cheer now ban - ish sad-ness, Je - sus' name glad lips em-ploy.
Heav'n takes up the won-drous sto - ry, Would the earth its splen-dor teach.
REFRAIN.
Wondrous name! Name of pow'r! Winning con - quests ev-'ry hour!
Wondrous name! Name of cheer! Deep'ning, wide'ning ev-'ry year;
Wondrous name! glo-ri-ous Name! Thro' e - ter - nal years the same;
Wondrous name! the earth it sways, Wakes new strains of joy and praise.
Hearts once broken, bowed, and sad, Now with heav'n-ly joy are glad.
Wondrous name! while angels sing, We our prais - es too would bring.
Rit.

108. ARE YOU COUNTING THE COST?

H. F. JAMES. D. E. DORTCH.

1. As you strive for the world, for its fame and its joy, Have you
2. In the crav - ing for wealth, for its glit - ter and show, In - to
3. Leave the rich - es of earth, seek the treas-ures a - bove, And thro'
care-ful - ly count-ed the cost? Is the prize rich e-nough all your
grief and de-spair you are cast; And you know not the peace heav'n a -
years that un-ceas - ing - ly roll, Heavenly powers shall be yours, with the
strength to em-ploy, When to win it the soul must be lost?
lone can be-stow, While your soul will be lost at the last!
full - ness of love, And the life, end - less life of the soul!
CHORUS.
Are you care-ful - ly counting the cost, Have you thought what it
count-ing the cost?
means to be lost, For the joys that decline do you
to be lost?

ARE YOU COUNTING THE COST? Concluded.

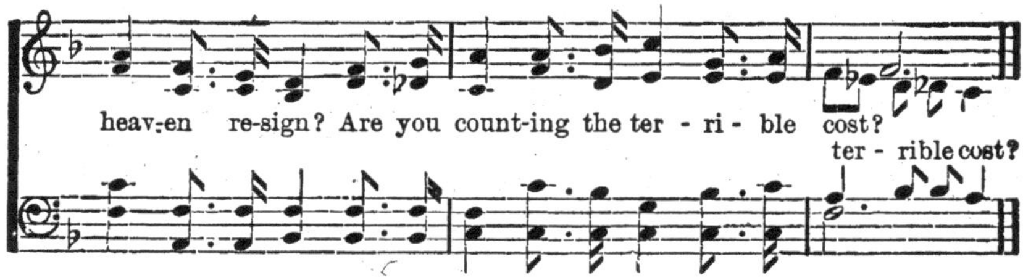
heav-en re-sign? Are you count-ing the ter - ri - ble cost?
ter - rible cost?

109. LESSON FOR ETERNITY.

E. D. M. E. S. LORENZ.

INFANT CLASS.
1. Oh, what a les-son we all may learn, Won-der-ful love of Christ!
2. Full-ness of blessing, of peace, and joy, Won-der-ful love of Christ!
3. In - to this truth, let the chil-dren in, Won-der-ful love of Christ!
INSTRUMENT.
Glad-ly our minds to its mes-sage turn, Won-der-ful love of Christ!
Sounding its depths shall our life em-ploy, Won-der-ful love of Christ!
Knowledge divine would we ev - er win, Won-der-ful love of Christ!
SCHOOL.
Tru - er knowledge ne'er can be; Deep-er truth they ne'er shall see;
Les - son for e - ter - ni - ty, Wonderful love of Christ!

110. LEANING ON THE EVERLASTING ARMS.

REV. E. A. HOFFMAN. A. J. SHOWALTER.

1. What a fel-lowship, what a joy di-vine, Leaning on the Ev-er-last-ing Arms! What a bless-ed-ness, what a peace is mine, Lean-ing on the Ev-er-last-ing Arms!
2. Oh, how sweet to walk in this pilgrim way, Leaning on the Ev-er-last-ing Arms! Oh how bright the path grows from day to day,
3. What have I to dread, what have I to fear, Leaning on the Ev-er-last-ing Arms! I have peace complete with my Lord so near,
REFRAIN.
Lean - - ing, lean - ing, Safe and secure from all a-larms; Lean - ing, Lean - - ing, Lean-ing on the Ev-er-last-ing Arms.
Lean-ing on Je-sus, Lean-ing on Je-sus, Leaning on Je-sus, Lean-ing on Je-sus,

111. LIFE AND LIGHT.

REV. T. W. BARBER. E. S. FOGG

1. My soul is joy-ful in the Lord, His light shines all a-round;
2. His blood has cleans'd me from all sin, I'm ev-'ry whit made whole;
3. My life is hid with Christ in God; My bread is in his word;
4. I care not for this world be-low, It has no charms I love;
For Je-sus is my life, my way, His love and grace a-bound.
The fount-ain of e-ter-nal life Wells up with-in my soul.
My meat and drink to do his will, For he doth grace af-ford.
I live by faith and faith a-lone, I seek a home a-bove.
CHORUS.
I am walk - - ing, walk-ing in the light, The
I am walk-ing, walk-ing,
beau-ti-ful light a-long the way, I am walk-ing,
a-long the way; I am walk-ing, walking,
walk-ing in the light, The beau-ti-ful light of God each day.

112. STAND THEREFORE.

PRISCILLA J. OWENS. E. S. LORENZ.

1. What ar-mor must he wear, What weapons must he bear, Who comes to do and dare In his youth? O wrap his heart a-round The gir-dle, firm-ly bound, Where rent is never found God's own truth.
2. Then put your ar-mor on, The bat-tle must be won, And gal-lant deeds be done, Life to gain. But truth your heart shall gird, You bear a conqu'rer's sword; Then onward pass the wor(, "Christ shall reign."
3. Then keep your ar-mor bright, Strike boldly for the right, Strive with all man-ly might, In his name. Be steadfast un-to death, Hold fast the shield of faith, And with your latest breath Vic-t'ry claim.
4. Be faith-ful to the last, Thro' ev-'ry-thing stand fast, Let fier-y darts be cast All in vain; For when the strife is o'er, Up-on the gold-en shore, With Christ forev-ermore You shall reign.
LEADER ONLY.
Stand there-fore,
CHORUS.
Hav-ing your loins girt a-bout with truth, (with truth,) And hav-ing on the breast-plate of right-eous-ness; And your

STAND THEREFORE. Concluded.

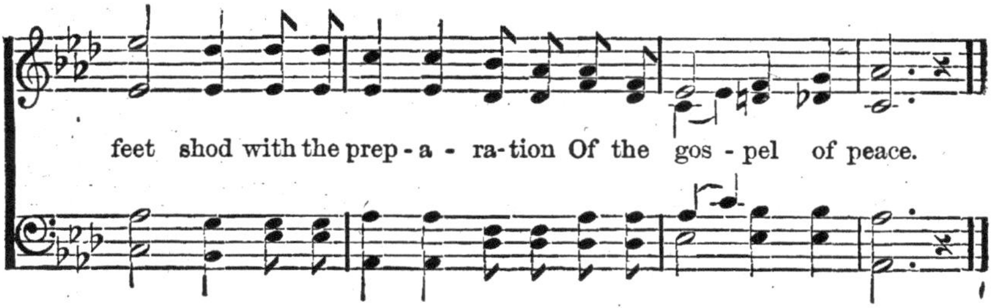
feet shod with the prep - a - ra-tion Of the gos - pel of peace.

113. ENOUGH FOR ME.

E. A. H. REV. E. A. HOFFMAN.

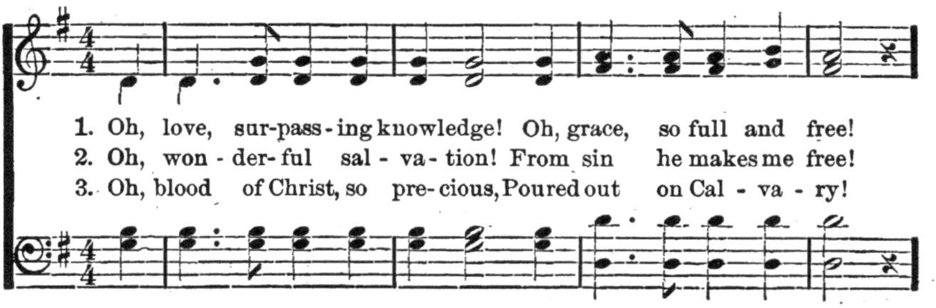
1. Oh, love, sur-pass-ing knowledge! Oh, grace, so full and free!
2. Oh, won - der-ful sal - va- tion! From sin he makes me free!
3. Oh, blood of Christ, so pre- cious, Poured out on Cal - va - ry!

FINE.
I know that Je - sus loves me, And that's enough for me.
I feel the sweet as - sur - ance, And that's enough for me.
I feel its cleansing pow - er, And that's enough for me.

D. S.
And that's e-nough for me, Oh, that's e-nough for me.

By permission.

114. ENTER THE PEARLY GATES.

M. B. S. — M. B. SIMON.

Moderato.

1. Hark to the words that once were spo - ken, Of a grand cit - y built a - bove, And of its streets all shin - ing brill - iant - ly with gold.
2. Turn from the gates that stand wide o - pen, Lead - ing from streets so great and broad, Thro' which the ma - ny care - less - ly do en - ter in.
3. Christ hath pre - pared the way so clear - ly, Free - ly for all, both great and small; Then do not tar - ry long - er to ac - cept his love;
Strait is the gate by which they en - ter, Nar - row the way by which they go, And but a few that safe - ly reach the fold.
Oft' they've been told to roam no long - er Where there are dan - gers great un - seen, Yet they will reap the hard wag - es of sin.
Grace he will give you in the jour - ney, Ten - der - ly watch so you'll not fall, Giv - ing you hope and peace and joy and love.

ENTER THE PEARLY GATES. Concluded.

CHORUS.
En-ter the gates, ... the beauti-ful gates, ...
En-ter the gates, beau-ti-ful gates,
En-ter the pearl-y gates While o-pen wide they stand . . . .
en-ter the gates.
En-ter the gates, ... the beauti-ful gates, ...
En-ter the gates, beau-ti-ful gates,
En-ter the pearl-y gates, At Christ's com-mand, ...
En-ter the gates.

115. OH, THE JOY I FEEL.

M. F. NOBLE. D. E. DORTCH.

1. I will sing all day of the Saviour's love, That once brought him down from his home a - bove; All my sins he par-doned and set me free; Soon he'll take me home with him-self to be.
2. Oh, the day will come when we all shall stand, At the throne of God as a blood-washed band; What a bliss 'twill be our dear Lord to see, And to sing his praise thro' e - ter - ni - ty.
3. Will you come, dear friend; give the Lord your heart, Ere his spir - it grieved from your soul de - part; There are crowns in glo - ry a - wait - ing those Who in Christ the Sav - iour their trust re - pose.
CHORUS.
O the joy I feel, As I hum - bly kneel, At the Sav-iour's feet in com-mun-ion sweet! He has cleansed my soul from its

Controlled by D. E. Dortch.

guilt and sin, Glo-ry be to God! There is peace with - in.

116. SAVIOUR, I COME.

REV. W. F. McCAULEY. E. S. LORENZ.

1. Wea - ry with want and sin, Long-ing and griev-ing, Feel-ing no
2. Mem-'ry the past re-views, My con - dem - na-tion; Now comes the
3. Tear drops of sor-row dumb, Heav-y and burn-ing, Jew - els of
4. Cour-age! no gloom-y past My soul shall sev - er; Hail to the
REFRAIN.
peace with-in—Earth's vain joys leav-ing,
glor-ious news, Christ my sal - va-tion!
light be-come, Eyes heav'nward turning.
joys that last Ev - er and ev - er.
Sav-iour, I come!
Now I come to thee,
Sav-iour, I come! Thou wilt give rest And bring me home.
Sav - iour! I come to thee!

117. JUST BEYOND THE RIVER.

FRED WOODROW. T. C. O'KANE.

1. There's a cit - y bright and fair, Just be-yond, beyond the riv - er,
2. Sin and sor - row are no more, Just be-yond, beyond the riv - er,
3. There we shall with Je - sus meet, Just be-yond, beyond the riv - er,
4. In that cit - y bright and fair, Just be-yond, beyond the riv - er,
All are good and hap - py there, Just be-yond, beyond the riv - er;
Death comes not up - on the shore, Just be-yond, beyond the riv - er;
And the good in glo - ry greet, Just be-yond, beyond the riv - er;
All at last may gath - er there, Just be-yond, beyond the riv - er;
Streets of gold are shin - ing bright, An - gels walk the plains of light,
None are sad with want or care, Pain or sick - ness none shall bear,
Lives whose tale no tongue has told, Men of God and saints of old,
We may meet to part no more,—All our troub - les will be o'er,
FINE.
And there nev - er com - eth night, Just be-yond, beyond the riv - er.
All are hap - py "o - ver there," Just be-yond, beyond the riv - er.
Mar - tyrs with their crowns of gold, Just be-yond, beyond the riv - er.
When we reach that "shining shore," Just be-yond, beyond the riv - er.

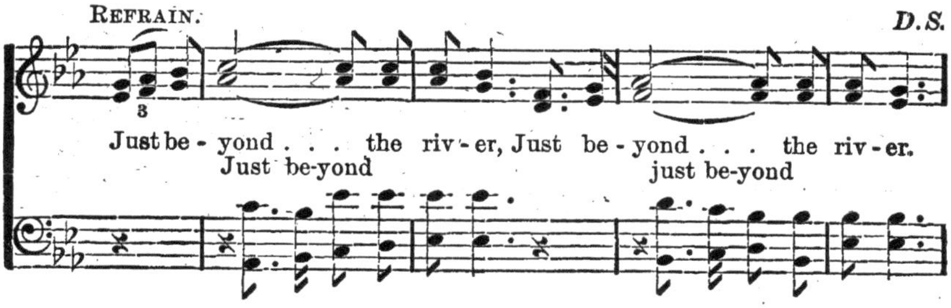
REFRAIN.
D.S.
Just be - yond . . . the riv - er, Just be - yond . . . the riv - er.
Just be-yond just be-yond

118. THE GLAD HEREAFTER.

(For Male Voices.)

JENNIE WILSON. E. S. LORENZ.

1. When passed are tears and laugh - ter And earth - ly gloom and glow,
2. Now oft - en-times his lead - ings Are where deep shad - ows lie,
3. Each chas - ten - ing af - flic - tion Is sent in ten - der love;
4. Though now tears flow un - bid - den, Here - af - ter we shall say,
FINE.
We shall in the here - af - ter The Mas - ter's deal-ings know.
And to our pray'r-ful plead - ings There seem - eth no re - ply.
And bears a ben - e - dic - tion, Down-waft-ed from a - bove.
Our Saviour's hand though hid - den, Has led us all the way.
D. S.—And a fade - less crown of glo - ry shall Suc - ceed the cross of pain.
CHORUS.
D. S.
In the light . . . . In the light . . . . . .
of the great hereaf - ter, life's dark paths shall be made plain,

119. LIGHT AND DARKNESS.

REV. GEO. MATHESON, D. D.

1. Lights in the up - per dwell-ing, Darkness in rooms be - low;
2. Each cross in earth's cre - a - tion, Beams in a star a - bove;
3. Therefore, O heav'nly Fa - ther, Lift I mine eyes to thee,
Harps in the high halls swell-ing, Si-lence where time-flow'rs grow;
Each sigh of man's pros-tra - tion Moves in God's harp of love;
What time a cloud shall gath-er Ov - er my hu - man sea:
Songs in the heav'nly mansions, Sighs in the low - er air;
Each tear of hearts made ten-der By the deep folds of night
Dark to my sight ap - pear-ing, Yet there is light some-where,
Crowns in the space ex - pan-sions, Cross-es in homes of care.
Sparkles with rainbow splen-dor, Rays of the Fa-ther's light.
Fraught with a mes-sage cheer-ing Those in the up - per air.
REFRAIN.
Un - til our lives are end-ed, Darkness and light are blen-ded;

Both from above de-scend-ed, Tell-ing of God's dear care.

120. WORDS OF SPIRIT AND LIFE.

REV. J. B. ATCHINSON. D. E. DORTCH.

1. Pre-cious words, I love to hear, Words of spir-it and life;
2. They who hear his words re - joice, Words of spir-it and life;
3. Wind and wave his will o - bey, Words of spir-it and life;
4. At death's riv - er I will hear, Words of spir-it and life;

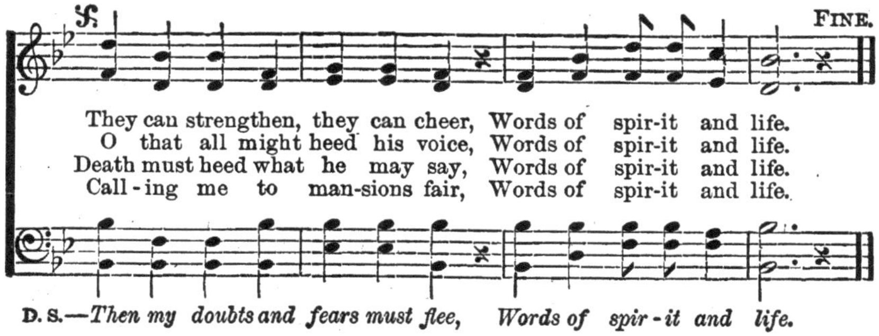
FINE.
They can strengthen, they can cheer, Words of spir-it and life.
O that all might heed his voice, Words of spir-it and life.
Death must heed what he may say, Words of spir-it and life.
Call - ing me to man-sions fair, Words of spir-it and life.
D. S.—Then my doubts and fears must flee, Words of spir - it and life.

D.S.
Bless-ed Je-sus hear my plea, Speak those words of life to me,

SOWING TIME.

ADALINE H. BERRY. C. D. AMSTUTZ.

1. See, the morn is bright'ning, In the east-ern sky; Up! for work make
2. Sow the seeds of kind-ness In your neighbor's heart; You will soon with
3. Sow a-long the high-way, Strangers may be there; You may make them
read - y, Lie not i - dly by; Has - ten to the grain-fields,
glad - ness See the plant-lets start; If the soil is sto - ny,
bet - ter By a gift or pray'r; Sow be-neath the noon - tide,
With your precious seed; Ma - ny will-ing workmen, Yet the Lord will need.
Nev - er fear to sow; Some rift may be o-pen, Where the stalk may grow,
While your strength is giv'n, Sow till life is end - ed, You will reap in heav'n.
CHORUS.
'Tis . . . . . . the time for sow - - ing Seeds . . . . . of
'Tis the time for sow - ing Seeds of precious worth, 'Tis the time for sow -

By permission.

SOWING TIME. Concluded.

prec-ious worth; . . . . . . Scat - - - - ter them like
ing Seeds of pre-cious worth, Scat- ter them like sun - shine,
sun - - shine O - - - - ver all the earth . . . . .
O - ver all the earth, Scatter them like sun - shine, O - ver all the earth.
'Tis . . . . . the time for sow - - ing Seeds . . . . . of
'Tis the time for sow - ing Seeds of precious worth, 'Tis the time for sow -
pre-cious worth, ... Scat - - - - - ter them like
ing Seeds of pre-cious worth; Scat- ter them like sun - shine,
sun - - shine, O - - - - ver all the earth. . . . . .
O-ver all the earth, Scatter them like sunshine, O - ver all the earth.

122. WE SHALL REST AT THE FOUNTAIN.

D. E. D. — D. E. DORTCH.

1. There's a fount-ain free flow-ing 'neath life's tree, We shall rest at the fountain by and by; There the hap-py soul nev-er shall grow old, We shall rest at the fount-ain by and by.
2. There's a fount-ain bright in that land of light, We shall rest at the fountain by and by; On its banks are flow'rs growing 'mid heav'ns bow'rs, We shall rest at the fount-ain by and by.
3. There's a fount-ain sweet where we all shall meet, We shall rest at the fountain by and by; Songs of joy we'll raise to our Sav-iour's praise, We shall rest at the fount-ain by and by.
4. There's a fount-ain free, sin-ner, 'tis for thee, We shall rest at the fountain by and by; Will you meet me there and its bless-ings share? We shall rest at the fount-ain by and by.
D. S.—There we all shall stand with the an-gel band, We shall rest at the fount-ain by and by.
Fine.
Refrain.
We shall rest at the fount-ain by and by, (by and by,)
We shall rest at the fount-ain by and by, (by and by;)
D. S.

By permission.

123. I AM SHELTERED IN THEE.

F. M. D. FRANK M. DAVIS.

1. I am safe in the Rock that is high - er than I; This my
2. I am safe in the Cleft that was riv - en for me; From the
3. I am safe in the Rock and what ev - er be - tide Death and
ref - uge thro' storms e'er shall be; Ma - ny barks are there tossed on the
pow'r of the tempt - er I'm free; Tho' my path - way be dark and the
hell have no ter - ror to me; I can walk with - out fear thro' the
bil - lows' mad foam, But I'm shel - tered for - ev - er in thee.
storms sweep the sky, Yet se - cure - ly I'm shel - tered in thee.
shad - ow - y vale, For se - cure - ly I'm shel - tered in thee.
CHORUS.
Shel - tered in thee, Shel - tered in thee, O thou
Shel - tered in thee, in thee,
blest Rock of A - ges, I am shel - tered in thee.

124. HOW YOU GROW.

FOR INFANT CLASS.

D. E. DORTCH.

Question. SOLO.
1. How do lit - tle bird- ies grow, Fly-ing, chirp-ing, sing-ing so?
2. How do lit - tle fish - es grow, Swimming, playing to and fro?
3. How do lit - tle children grow? Not by drinking rum I know;
Are they fed with wine and rum, In their daint-y nest - ing home?
Do they live in bran-dy streams, As they glide 'neath sun-ny beams?
Bran-dy, ci - der, wine, and beer Nev - er make them strong and fair.
Answer. DUET.
No, no, no, no, Let me tell you, no, no, no, no, no, Wa-ter makes the
No, no, no, no, Let me tell you, no, no, no, no, no, Wa-ter makes the
No, no, no, no, Let me tell you, no, no, no, no, no, Wa-ter makes the
FULL CHORUS.
bird - ies grow; Rain drops patter, dew drops scatter, So the fresh and
fish - es grow; Rain drops patter, dew drops scatter, Brooks and riv -ers
child-ren grow; Rain drops patter, dew drops scatter, Fountains fill and
cooling water Wets their ti-ny beaks and lo! This is how the bird-ies grow.
flow with water, Where they live and thrive, and lo! This is how the fish-es grow.
flow with water, See they bathe and drink and lo! This is how the children grow.

By permission.

125. LOOKOUT SONG.

W. F. McCAULEY. W. F. McCAULEY.

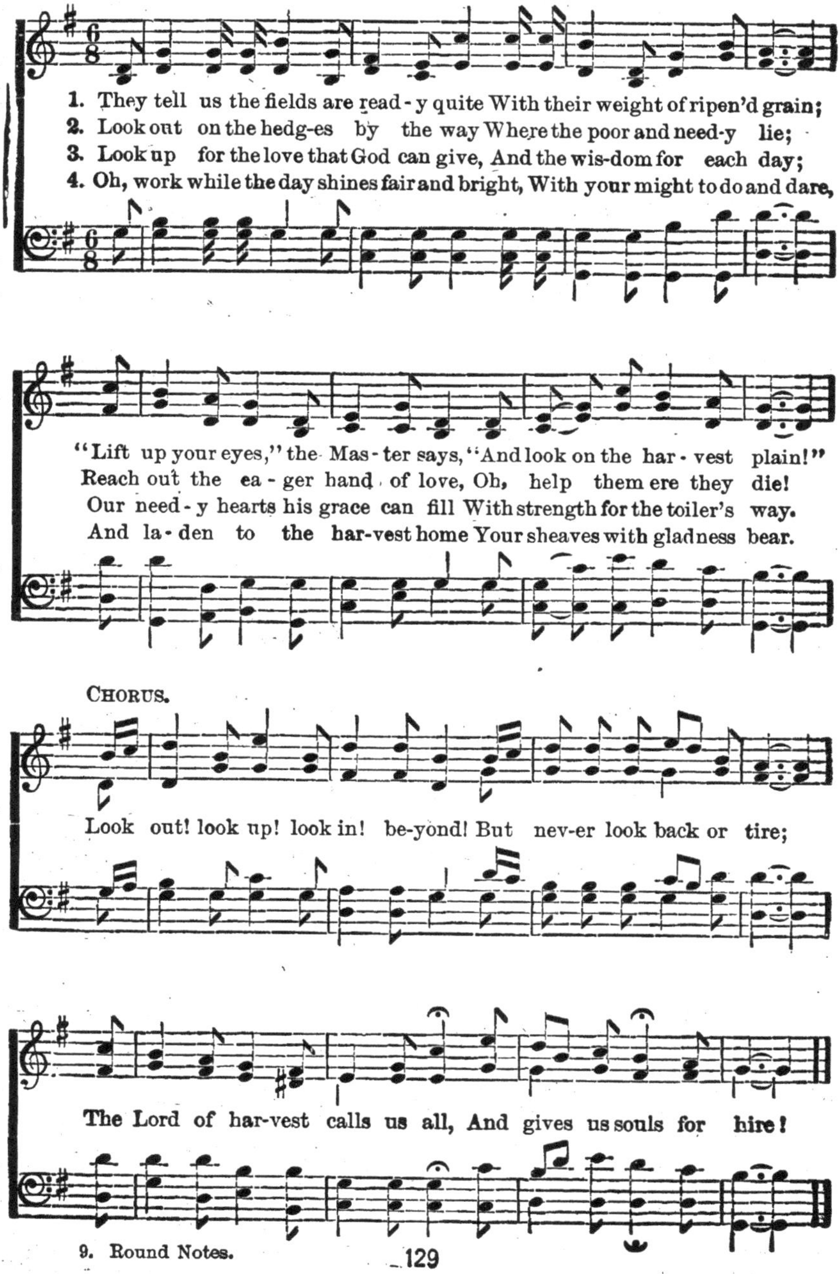
1. They tell us the fields are read - y quite With their weight of ripen'd grain;
2. Look out on the hedg-es by the way Where the poor and need-y lie;
3. Look up for the love that God can give, And the wis-dom for each day;
4. Oh, work while the day shines fair and bright, With your might to do and dare,
"Lift up your eyes," the Mas - ter says, "And look on the har - vest plain!"
Reach out the ea - ger hand of love, Oh, help them ere they die!
Our need - y hearts his grace can fill With strength for the toiler's way.
And la - den to the har-vest home Your sheaves with gladness bear.
CHORUS.
Look out! look up! look in! be-yond! But nev-er look back or tire;
The Lord of har-vest calls us all, And gives us souls for hire!

LEARN OF JESUS.

E. D. MUND. REV. ISAIAH BALTZELL.

1. Are you seek-ing for the truth? Learn of Je- sus! Yield your mind to Him in
2. Bowing low- ly at his feet, Learn of Je- sus! He has les-sons rare and
3. Are you stumbling, weak, and blind? Learn of Jesus! He is gen-tle, true, and
4. Deep-er vis-ion he will give, Learn of Je- sus! Larg-er life you then will
youth, Learn of Je - sus! Wise is he beyond our thought, Knowing
sweet, Learn of Je - sus! Life will rich- er treasure show, Earth with
kind, Learn of Je - sus! He will lead in wisdom's way, Fill with
live, Learn of Je - sus! He will sat - is - fy your soul, And his
all things we have sought; Wealth of wisdom he has brought, Learn of Je- sus!
heav'nly light will glow; Deeper truth will he be-stow, Learn of Je - sus!
light your darkest day, By your side will ev- er stay, Learn of Je - sus!
truth will make you whole; Would you reach life's truest goal? Learn of Je - sus!
CHORUS.
Learn of Je - - - - sus! Learn of Je - - - sus!
Learn of Je- sus! ev- 'ry day; At his feet for - ev - er stay,
Learn of Je - - - - sus! Learn of Je - - - sus!
Learn of Je- sus! ea ger - ly, Les - sons for e - ter- ni - ty!

Earth-ly wis-dom can but fail; Heav'n-ly wis-dom must pre-vail
O'er life's sor-rows, in death's vale, Learn of Je-sus!

127. CHILDREN OF THE HEAVENLY KING.

JOHN CENNICK. AMERICAN MELODY.

1. Chil-dren of the heav'n-ly King, As we jour-ney let us sing,
2. Fear not, brethren, joy-ful stand On the bor-ders of our land;
Fine.
Sing our Sav-iur's worth-y praise, Glo-rious in his works and ways.
Je-sus Christ, our Father's Son, Bids us un-dis-mayed go on.
D. S.—They are hap-py now, and we Soon their hap-pi-ness shall see.
On-ly thou our lead-er be, And we still will fol-low thee.
D.S.
We are trav'ling home to God In the way our fa-thers trod;
Lord! o-bed-ient-ly we'll go, Glad-ly leav-ing all be-low;

128. SHOULDER TO SHOULDER.

H. F. JAMES. E. S. LORENZ.

1. Shoul-der to shoul-der, the face to the foe, Firm and u-nit-ed, right
2. Ten-der the ties that our hearts firm u-nite: Love to our Lord, to his
3. O'er all the land now the foe we en-gage, Why should we fear, tho' he
on-ward we go; Not in our mighty host—This is our on-ly boast,
word full of light; Love for his fal-len ones, Care for his er-ring ones,
men-ace and rage? Wielding the sword of truth, Knowing for wrong no ruth,
CHORUS.
This cheers and nerves us most, God leads us on.
Joy, that as lov-ing sons, God owns us all.
God claims our pow'r and youth, He leads us on.
Shoulder to shoulder we
on-ward go to vic-to-ry! Firm and u-nit-ed, our God with us, the
foe must flee; Clad in God's pan-o-ply we on-ward go.

129. HIS LEADING HAND.

DR. S. FILLMORE BENNETT. CHAS. H. GABRIEL.

1. How oft this heart of mine Has been be-set by fears: How oft these
2. How of-ten have the clouds Hung heavy o'er my way, When scarce a
3. Why should I be a-fraid When such a friend is near, Or mur-mur
weeping eyes Have flowed with bitter tears: Yet, ev-en when to sight Rose
sunbeam came To bless the drea-ry day. Yet, al-ways, ere my soul Quite
at the cross I may be called to bear? Nay, be my trust in Him Whose
dangers strange and new, And waters closed around, His hand has led me through.
faint-ed in the night, His lov-ing hand appeared To lead me to the light.
grace is free to all, Who guides with loving hand, What ever may be-fall.
CHORUS.
His hand has led me, His hand has led me
His hand has led, has led me through, His hand has led me, led me through,
His hand has led, has led me through, And still is lead-ing me.

130. LET US PAY OUR VOWS.

E. D. MUND. E. S. LORENZ.

1. { We have entered roy - al ser-vice, pledged our utmost pow'r, We have
{ His commands we heed with gladness, ev - 'ry day and hour, We have
2. { There are words of praise and hon-or we are pledged to speak, We have
{ Tho' our speech be slow and stamm'ring, and our hearts be weak, We have
3. { There is light we must be seek-ing in his ho - ly word, We have
{ There are hid - den words of com-fort that we have not heard, We have
4. { Oh, the joy of loy - al ser - vice, oh, the ten - der grace, When we
{ We shall walk in white be-fore him, see his lov - ing face, If we
made our vows un-to the Lord! made our vows un-to the Lord!
made our vows un-to the Lord! made our vows un-to the Lord!
made our vows un-to the Lord! made our vows un-to the Lord!
pay our vows un-to the Lord! pay our vows un-to the Lord!
CHORUS.
Let us pay our vows un-to the Lord, (un-to the Lord.) Let us pay our vows
un - to the Lord, (un - to the Lord!) Now in the presence of his
peo - ple Let us pay our vows un - to the Lord!

131. EXALT THE NAME OF JESUS.

JENNIE WILSON. I. BALTZELL.

1. Ex - alt the name of Je - sus, All - oth - er names a - bove;
2. Ex - alt the name of Je - sus, By yield - ing, glad and free,
3. Ex - alt the name of Je - sus, By lov - ing la - bor wrought;
4. Ex - alt the name of Je - sus, Till earth scenes pass a - way;
No oth - er word by mor - tals heard So claims a - dor - ing love.
To him thy heart, and all thou art, For - ev - er his to be.
And strive from sin for Christ to win Dear souls his blood has bought.
And then on high still glo - ri - fy Our Sav - iour's name for aye.
CHORUS.
Ex - alt the ho - ly, sav - ing name, Which un - to us is giv'n,
Where-by to gain e - ter - nal life, And end - less joy in heav'n.

132. READY FOR THE MASTER.

W. F. McCAULEY. W. F. McCAULEY.

1. My heart has a bur - den of joy to - day—Read - y when the
2. But should he command me to lin - ger still—Read - y till the
3. The path may be rough, and the strife be long—Read - y where the
4. Though sin - ful and weak, yet his voice I hear—Read - y! for the
Mas - ter shall call me! I am walk - ing now in the
Mas - ter shall call me! I'll re - joice to serve at his
Mas - ter shall call me! There's a crown at last and a
Mas - ter doth call me! By his sav - ing love I can
heav'n- ward way, Read - y when the Mas - ter shall call me.
ho - ly will, Read - y till the Mas - ter shall call me.
glad new song, Read - y where the Mas - ter will call me.
come, nor fear, Read - y as the Mas - ter doth call me.
Refrain.
Read-y now, O bless - ed Mas - ter, Serving thee no ill shall be - fall me;
Read-y for the Master, tell-ing me to-day, "In-to love and mercy I call thee!"

133. SOME DAY.

E. E. REXFORD. FRANK M. DAVIS.

DUET.
Slow, with expression.
1. I hear a song, a song so sweet, I try all vain - ly to re-peat,
2. Some day my jour - ney will be done, Earth will be pass'd and heaven won;
3. "Some day" I say, con-tent to wait The opening of the Jas-per gate;
4. When comes the time for me to go, The homeward path I may not know,
Its mel - o - dy and feel-ing say, I'll sing it if God will some day.
And when the long rough way is trod, I shall be-hold the face of God.
Come soon or late that day will be The dawn of end - less rest to me.
But in God's hand my own I'll lay, And he will lead me home "some day."
CHORUS.
Some day, some hap - py day to be, My voice will learn its melo - dy.
Some happy day, a day to be My voice will learn its melody.
cres.
ritard.
And I shall sing the songs so sweet, Of rest and heav'n at Je-sus' feet.

By permission of the Author.

134. GRACE AND GLORY.

PRISCILLA J. OWENS. E. S. LORENZ.

1. My light and strength, . . . my sun and shield, ... How
2. The days are dark, ... the nights are long, ... But
3. No bless-ed gift . . . . . will he with-hold, ... If
can I do with-out thee? How soon my poor . . . . . .
Christ, my sun, is shin-ing; He teach-es me . . . .
I but walk up-right-ly; And when the deep . . . . . .
weak heart would yield. . . . Wert thou not close a-bout me:
a pre-cious song, ... While on his arm re-clin-ing.
black shades en-fold, ... His truth is shin-ing bright-ly;
But ev-ry day, ... the nar-row way . . . . . . Grows
My help and stay, ... not far a-way, ... But
And when foes stand . . . . . to bar my way, ... His
bright-er still be-fore me; The Lord sends grace . . . . .
con-stant watching o'er me. The Lord sends grace . . . . .
shield is spread be-fore me; His grace still keeps . . . . .

for ev-'ry day, ... And crowns the end with glo-ry.
for ev-'ry day, ... While march-ing on to glo-ry.
me day by day, ... And heav'n o'erflows with glory.

135. TELL IT ALL TO JESUS.

WILLIAM H. GARDNER. CHAS. H. GABRIEL.

1. When your heart is trou-bled, Lift to heav'n a prayer, Tell it all to
2. When the gold-en sun-shine Fills the way with light, Tell it all to
3. When death takes your lov'd ones, And your heart is sore, Tell it all to
Je-sus, He is list'ning there.
Je-sus, All your joys re-cite.
Jesus, He'll bring peace once more.
REFRAIN.
Tell it all to Je-sus, He will
give you rest; Tell it all to Je-sus, And you shall be blest.

136. WALK WITH THE SAVIOUR.

ANNA CHICHESTER. F. E. POWELL.

1. Walk with the Sav-iour, make his ways your choice; Know-ing his
2. Walk with the Sav-iour, keep-ing step with him, Fear-ing no
3. Walk with the Sav-iour, what tho' sor-row fall O-ver your
4. Walk with the Sav-iour, till your journey's end, Then with your
kind-ness, your soul may well re-joice; Where can you find com-
dan-ger, nor dreading foe-man grim: Tho' with his le-gions
soul like a gloomy, heav-y pall! Sor-row must come, but
Lord an e-ter-ni-ty you'll spend; Here in the dark-ness,
pan-ion-ship more sweet? Where find a friendship that's so com-plete?
Sa-tan may ap-pear, You need not wa-ver, with Je-sus near.
Je-sus com-fort gives; Hap-py the soul that with him e'er lives.
there you'll rest in light; Sor-row and woe will have tak-en flight.
CHORUS.
Walk with the Sav-iour! Hark! he in-
Walk with the Sav-iour! walk with the Sav-iour! Hark! he in-

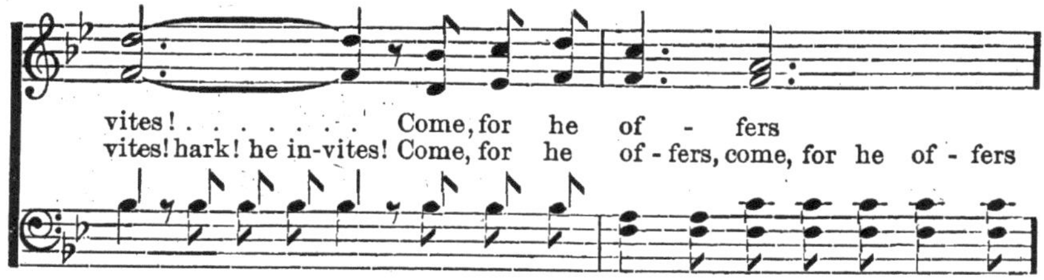
vites! . . . . Come, for he of - fers
vites! hark! he in-vites! Come, for he of - fers, come, for he of - fers

End-less de - lights. . . . . . Why do you lin - ger,
End-less delights, endless delights. Why do you lin-ger, why do you lin-ger,

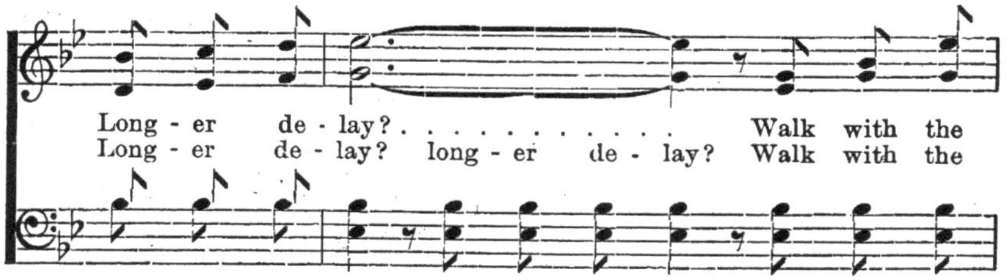
Long - er de - lay? . . . . Walk with the
Long - er de - lay? long - er de - lay? Walk with the

Sav - iour, Join him to - day! . . . . . .
Sav-iour, walk with the Saviour, Join him to - day! join him to-day!

137. BENEDICTION.

I. THESS. 5: 28. E. S. LORENZ.

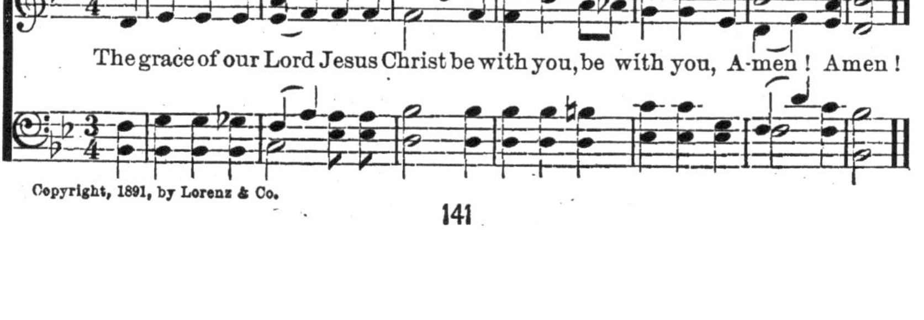
The grace of our Lord Jesus Christ be with you, be with you, A-men! Amen!

138. SATISFIED WITH JESUS.

ANNA CHICHESTER. JOHN TIBBALLS.

1. { I am walk - ing with the Sav - iour in the bless - ed nar - row way, I am sat - is - fied with Christ, my Lord; }
{ Once my soul was in the dark - ness, now has dawn'd life's gold - en day, I am sat - is - fied with Christ, my Lord. }
D. S.—nev - er will for - sake me, but will ev - er be my guide, I am sat - is - fied with Christ, my Lord.
FINE.
CHORUS.
I am sat - is - fied, with Je - sus yes, I am sat - is - fied, with Je - sus,
I am sat - is - fied to walk with him the long, long way; For he
D. S.

2 In my griefs he's consolation, and in
trial he's my stay,
I am satisfied with Christ my Lord;
With his tender arms around me I can
never know dismay,
I am satisfied with Christ, my Lord.

3 When I falter in my weakness, on his
arm he bids me lean,
I am satisfied with Christ, my Lord;
When temptation overwhelms me, with
his blood he makes me clean,
I am satisfied with Christ, my Lord.

4 I am happy in his service, I rejoice in
God, my King,
I am satisfied with Christ, my Lord;
For each day he opens treasures, gives
new songs of joy to sing,
I am satisfied with Christ, my Lord.

5 Oh, the words of love and comfort! Oh,
the tender loving hand!
I am satisfied with Christ, my Lord;
Through the waters it will lead me to
the fair Lamb-lighted land,
I am satisfied with Christ, my Lord.

139. COME UNTO ME.

ANNA SHARE. E. S. LORENZ.

1. Sweet-ly the Sav-iour's voice is ev - er call - ing, Come un - to me!
2. Long have I sought you, lost in darkness drear-y, Come un - to me!
3. Here is the rest that I a-lone can give you, Come un - to me!
4. Je - sus, for-sak - ing all that would deceive us, Come we to thee;
Come un - to me! See shad-ows dark a-round you now are fall - ing,
Come un - to me! I am the ref - uge, wait - ing for the wea - ry,
Come un - to me! Come, for my heart is long - ing to for - give you,
Come we to thee! Safe in thy lov - ing arms, O Lord, re - ceive us,
CHORUS.
Come un - to me!
Come un - to me!
Come un - to me!
Com - ing to thee!
Je - sus, the Lord of all, Oh, hear his lov - ing call,
Come un - to me, all ye wea - ry ones, O come! Come un - to me!
Come un - to me! Come, all ye wea - ry ones, no lon - ger roam.

140. GOD BE WITH YOU.

REV. J. E. RANKIN, D. D., LL.D. W. G. TOMER.

1. God be with you till we meet a - gain; By his counsels guide, up-hold you, With his sheep se-cure-ly fold you, God be with you
2. God be with you till we meet a - gain, 'Neath his wings se-cure-ly hide you; Dai - ly man-na still di - vide you, God be with you
3. God be with you till we meet a - gain; When life's per-ils thick con-found you, Put his arms un-fail-ing round you, God be with you
4. God be with you till we meet a - gain; Keep love's banner floating o'er you, Smite death's threatening wave be-fore you, God be with you
till we meet a - gain,
CHORUS.
Till we meet, . . . till we meet,
Till we meet, till we meet a - gain,
Till we meet at Je - sus' feet,
Till we meet;
Till we meet, . .
Till we meet,
till we meet,
till we meet a - gain,
God be with you till we meet a - gain.

141. MAKE IT A FULL SALVATION.

E. R. LATTA. J. H. RUEBUSH.

1. Je - sus, I own thy par - don, Tak - ing my guilt a - way!
2. Brok-en the bonds of Sa - tan, Gone are my guilt - y fears!
3. Gone is thy right- eous an - ger! Sweet - ly thy face hath smiled!
4. Patience and hope, un- fail- ing, Un - to thy ser - vant give!
Gone is the blind - ing dark-ness, Gone is my soul's dis - may!
Spok- en thy words of mer - cy, Dry - ing a - way my tears!
Bless - ed, the Spir - it's wit - ness, Own - ing me as thy child!
Faith that will nev - er wav - er, Let me from Thee re - ceive!
Make it a full sal - va - tion! Let me thy full - ness prove!
Make it a full sal - va - tion! Grant a com - plete re - lease!
Make it a full sal - va - tion! Roots of my sin de - stroy!
All that thy word re - quir - eth, Let it be done in me!
Make it a full sal - va - tion! Per - fect my soul in love!
Make it a full sal - va - tion! Per - fect my soul in peace!
Purge me to snow - y white-ness! Per - fect my soul in joy!
Make it a full sal - va - tion! Per - fect me, Lord, in thee!

142. LINGER NOT.

JENNIE WILSON. D. E. DORTCH.

1. Lin - ger not, the Lord is call - ing, Sin-ner friend, will you o - bey?
2. Lin - ger not, the Lord is call - ing, Ye who id - ly wait-ing stand,
3. Lin - ger not, the Lord is call - ing, Go and cheer some stricken heart,
4. Lin - ger not, the Lord is call - ing, Go and tell the sto - ry sweet,
5. Lin - ger not, the Lord is call - ing, Go wher-ev - er he may lead,
Cross the line in - to his king-dom, Heed his pleading voice to-day.
In the Master's world-wide vineyard There is work for ev - 'ry hand.
In his name to grief-bound spir-its Christian hope and rest im-part.
Un - to souls in sin and dark-ness Je - sus' lov - ing call re - peat.
Seek - ing in his stead to light - en, Hu-man sor - row, sin and need.
CHORUS.
Lin - ger not, lin - ger not, heed the Mas-ter's call, Lin - ger not,
Lin - ger not, lin - ger not, there is work for all, Lin - ger not,
lin - ger not, heed the Mas-ter's call!
lin - ger not, (Omit. . . . .) There is work for all.
1
2

143. GIVE, FREELY GIVE.

E. D. MUND.

E. S. LORENZ.

1. "Give !" says the earth, as her fruit she yields, "Give, free - ly give !"
2. "Give !" say the clouds, as earth's thirst they slake, "Give, free - ly give !"
3. "Give !" is the les - son of har - vest days, "Give, free - ly give !"
4. "Give !" says the gift, oth - er gifts a - bove, "Give, free - ly give !"
"Give !" is the voice of the gold - en fields, "Give, free - ly give!
"Give !" is the song brooks and streams a - wake, "Give, free - ly give!
"Give !" says the boun - ty that wakes our praise, "Give, free - ly give!
"Give !" says the God of a - bound - ing love, "Give, free - ly give!
CHORUS.
"Give!" is the cry of the joy - ous soul, "Bet - ter the part than the
unshared whole!" "Give!" let the gen - er - ous cho - rus roll, "Give, free - ly give!"

144. WE ARE READY.

EVA SMITH. D. E. DORTCH.

1. We're a hap-py pilgrim band, Marching on to Can'an's land, To that
2. We are hap-py all the day, Since he wash'd our sins a-way, And we'll
3. O ye wand'rers, quickly come And go with us to that home; If you
bright ce-les-tial home so far a-way; We are sav'd from guilt and sin,
serve our Sav-iour tru-ly to the end; Then a crown of joy we'll wear,
seek him he will save your soul from sin; Now for heav'n and glo-ry start,
And his spir-it dwells within, And we're ready for the Saviour when he comes.
In that home so bright and fair; We are read-y for the Saviour when he comes.
From the paths of vice de-part, And be ready for the Saviour when he comes.
Refrain.
When he comes, when he comes, We are
When the bless-ed Sav-iour comes, when the blessed Sav-iour comes,
read-y for the Saviour when he comes; When he comes,
When the bless-ed Saviour comes, When the

comes, We are read-y for the Saviour when he come,
bless-ed Saviour comes, when he comes.

145. JESUS, SAVIOUR, PILOT ME.

REV. EDWARD HOPPER. J. E. GOULD.

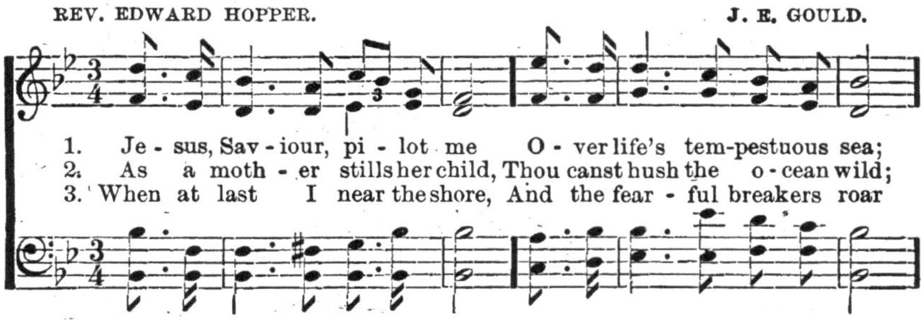
1. Je - sus, Sav - iour, pi - lot me O - ver life's tem-pestuous sea;
2. As a moth - er stills her child, Thou canst hush the o - cean wild;
3. When at last I near the shore, And the fear - ful breakers roar

Unknown waves be-fore me roll, Hid - ing rock, and treach'rous shoal;
Boist'rous waves o - bey thy will, When thou sayst to them, "Be still!"
'Twixt me and the peaceful rest; Then, while lean- ing on thy breast,

Chart and com - pass come from thee: Je - sus, Sav - iour, pi - lot me.
Wondrous Sov-'reign of the sea, Je - sus, Sav - iour, pi - lot me.
May I hear thee say to me, "Fear not, I will pi - lot thee!"

146. OVER THE WORLD.

E. D. MUND. E. S. LORENZ.

1. Let the light of life now shine O - ver the world! (o- ver the world!)
2. Bid the sun of right-eous-ness, O - ver the world! (o- ver the world!)
3. Speed the day when Christ shall reign O - ver the world! (o- ver the world!)
Beam with ra - di-ance di-vine O - ver the world! (o - ver the world!)
Rise the wait- ing lands to bless, O - ver the world! (o - ver the world!)
Truth can nev - er shine in vain O - ver the world! (o - ver the world!)
Send the word to lands ap - peal-ing, Scat - ter wide its leaves of heal-ing,
I - dol thrones are tott'ring, shaking, Pow'rs of dark-ness sore are quaking,
'Neath its beams fond hope is springing, Lands long dumb break in-to sing-ing,
Rit.
Love and life to all re - veal-ing, O - ver the world! o - ver the world!
As the light of life is breaking O - ver the world! o - ver the world!
Glad the notes of joy are ring-ing O - ver the world! o - ver the world!

By permission.

147. CLOSER THAN A BROTHER.

F. W. H. REV. F. W. HOOVER.

1. Oft - en in our jour-ney here, We're oppressed by doubt and fear, And the
2. Earth-ly friends may come and go, Fail when storms of trial blow, But this
3. In your hour of deep-est grief, He will sure-ly send re-lief, He is
cares of life our faith would almost smother; But there's One who lives above,
love a-bides when dis-ap-pears all oth - er; He will nev-er leave his own,
far more ten-der than the fond-est moth-er; On - ly good doth he in-tend,
D. S.—If you need a loy - al friend
One whose ver - y name is "Love," He's the Friend that stick-eth
Kind-ness hath he ev - er shown, He's the Friend that stick-eth
Trust him, he will still de-fend, He's the Friend that stick-eth
Who'll be with you till the end, Christ's the friend that stick-eth
FINE. CHORUS.
clos - er than a broth - er.
clos - er than a broth - er.
clos - er than a broth - er.
O that Friend! Tru - est
O that Friend!
clos - er than a broth - er.
D. S.
Friend! Friend to those that walk his ways and seek none oth-er;
tru - est Friend!

148. WHEN HE CALLS HIS CHILDREN HOME.

WM. H. GARDNER. EDWIN MOORE.

1. How our hearts will throb with gladness, When no more we have to roam.
2. How the air will ring with prais-es, As the gold-en streets they tread.
3 Then the Lord will bid his chil-dren, En - ter ev - er-last - ing rest,
Oh, how bright will be the morn - ing, When he calls his chil-dren home.
What a boun - teous, roy - al ban - quet, For the ransom'd will be spread.
And they'll dwell with him for-ev - er, In his wondrous mansions blest.
REFRAIN.
When our wea - ry wand'ring's o - ver And no more the earth we roam,
When our wear-y wand'ring's over, And no more the earth we roam,
There will be a great re- joic - ing, When he calls his chil-dren home.
There will be a great rejoic-ing,

149. SOW THE GOOD SEED.

E. D. MUND. E. S. LORENZ.

1. Youth is the seed time, and life is the field;
2. Har - vests of e - vil will fol - low your tares,
3. Bless - ing and hon - or the sow - er a - wait,
Sow the good seed! sow the good seed! What we are sow - ing its
Sow the good seed! sow the good seed! Shame and dis- grace e - vil
Sow - ing good seed! sow - ing good seed! Sheaves of re - joic - ing he'll
har - vest will yield; Sow the good seed! sow the good seed!
seed ev - er bears; Sow the good seed! sow the good seed!
bring to heav'n's gate; Sow - ing good seed! sow - ing good seed!
Chorus.
Har - vest days will come at last, Days of weep - ing soon be past;
At His feet our sheaves we'll cast, Grown from good seed! grown from good seed!

150. IN THE GLAD NEW TIME.

REV. GEO. MATHESON, D. D. E. S. LORENZ.

1. There are com-ing chang - es great In the glad new time, It is
2. We shall lift op - pres-sion's load In the glad new time, We shall
3. There shall be a might-y love In the glad new time, It shall
4. There shall be a joy in heav'n In the glad new time, For God's
worth our while to wait For the glad new time; Mountain fears shall prostrate lie,
bear the cross of God In the glad new time; We shall seek the valleys deep
come from heights above In the glad new time; It shall stoop with Christ below
rest-ing shall be giv'n In the glad new time; For his Sabbath shall be found,
Vales of hope be lift - ed high, Trembling earth embrace the sky,
Where the wear - y strive or sleep, And con - vey them up the steep,
To the path where sin-ners go, And shall gird them with the glow
When the skies have touch'd the ground, And the val - leys shall re-sound
CHORUS.
In the glad new time.
To the glad new time.
Of the glad new time.
With the glad new time.
In the glad . . . .
In the glad, the hap - py new time,
new time,
In the glad,
In the glad, the hap-py new time,
The happy new time,

IN THE GLAD NEW TIME. Concluded.

new time, Right shall win and e - vil shall fall,
In the glad, the hap-py new time,

God's dear will shall rule o - ver all, In the glad, in the glad new time.

151. SUN OF MY SOUL.

J. KEBLE. RITTER.

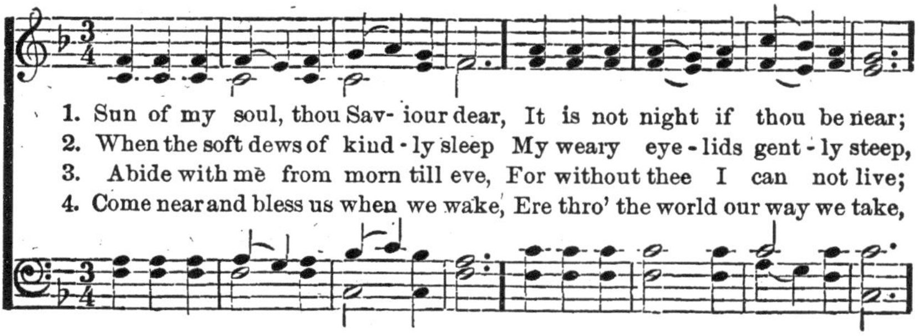
1. Sun of my soul, thou Sav- iour dear, It is not night if thou be near;
2. When the soft dews of kind - ly sleep My weary eye - lids gent - ly steep,
3. Abide with me from morn till eve, For without thee I can not live;
4. Come near and bless us when we wake, Ere thro' the world our way we take,

Oh, may no earth-born cloud a - rise To hide thee from thy serv-ant's eyes.
Be my last thought, how sweet to rest For ev-er on my Sav- iour's breast.
A-bide with me when night is nigh, For without thee I dare not die.
Till in the o - cean of - thy love We lose ourselves in heav'n a - bove.

152. TARRY WITH US.

REV. W. T. DALE. D. E. DORTCH.

1. Tar - ry with us,bless - ed Je - sus, For the ev'n - ing shad-ows fall;
2. Tar - ry with us, lov - ing Mas - ter, Till the morn - ing light ap - pears,
3. Here our hearts are press'd with sadness For our kin - dred gone be - fore,
And the day is fast re - ced - ing, Darkness gath - ers like a pall;
For we're pilgrims sad and lone - ly, Let thy pres-ence calm our fears;
Friends who now are watching for us, Wait - ing on the oth - er shore.
Tar - ry with us, bless - ed Sav - iour, For we're in a des - ert drear;
Tar - ry with us for we're pilgrims, Camping on a des - ert plain;
When we gath - er in the morn - ing, Morn - ing of e - ter - nal rest,
See the day of life is pass - ing, And the night of death is near.
All is lone - li - ness with - out thee, Gra - cious Mas - ter here re - main.
Shall we meet no more to sev - er, Be with Christ for - ev - er blest?
CHORUS.
Tar - ry with . . . . us, bless - ed Je - - - - sus,
Tar - ry with us, bless - ed Je - sus, tar - ry with us thro' the night;

Controlled by D. E. Dortch.

TARRY WITH US. Concluded.

Tar - ry till . . . . the morn-ing light;
Tar - ry with us, bless-ed Je - sus, tar - ry till the morn-ing light;
Tar - ry with . . . . us thro' the dark - - - ness,
Tar - ry with us thro' the dark-ness, tar - ry till the morn-ing light,
Tar - ry with us, bless - ed Je - sus, all the night (all the night).

153. COME, HOLY SPIRIT, HEAVENLY DOVE.

ISAAC WATTS. ADAPTED BY R. SIMPSON.

1. Come, Ho - ly Spir - it, heav'n-ly Dove! With all thy quick'ning pow'rs,—
2. Dear Lord! and shall we ev - er live At this poor dy - ing rate?
3. Come, Ho - ly Spir - it, heav'n-ly Dove! With all thy quick'ning powers,—
Kin-dle a flame of sa - cred love In these cold hearts of ours.
Our love so faint, so cold to thee, And thine to us so great.
Come, shed a-broad a Sav-iour's love, And that shall kin - dle ours.

154. **HARVEST PRAISE.**

E. D. MUND. E. S. LORENZ.

1. Wake the voice of gladness, praise the Lord to - day! Praise his ho - ly name!
2. Earth is filled with plenty by his ten- der care, Praise his ho - ly name!
3. All the earth is smiling, brings its si- lent praise, Praise his ho - ly name!
praise his ho-ly name! Filled with joy of har- vest, all his grace dis - play,
praise his ho-ly name! None need want or hun-ger, all his bless-ings share,
praise his ho-ly name! As you view his boun-ty, add your joy- ful lays,
Spread abroad his wondrous fame.
Praise ye him with hearts a-flame.
All his tender care pro-claim!
CHORUS.
To the Lord of Harvest bring sincerest praises;
Ev'ry heart re-joic - ing as its song it rais-es! Crowned with love and mercy,
with un-bounded grac-es, Praise the Lord of harvest, praise his ho - ly name!

155. JESUS IS MY JOY AND SONG.

Words arr. D. E. DORTCH.

1. On sin's dark mountain I had wandered far a - way; Blackness of
2. Oft-times I've listened To the sto - ry o'er and o'er; Heard Je-sus
3. Now I am hap-py For I feel the cleansing pow'r; On Je-sus
4. Come now to Je- sus, He will cleanse your soul from sin; Oh hear him
dark- ness Hid from me the light of day; My sins were heav - y
knock-ing, But I o - pened not the door; My sins were heav - y
lean- ing, Jour-ney with him hour by hour; My sins were heav - y
knock-ing, Let the bless- ed Sav-iour in; Your sins are heav - y
and my burdens hard to bear; But I went to Je-sus trusting and I
and my burdens hard to bear; But I went to Je-sus trusting and I
and my burdens hard to bear; But I went to Je-sus trusting and I
and your burdens hard to bear; If you come to Je-sus trusting you can
D. S.—I will go with him some day to dwell with
FINE.
CHORUS.
D.S.
left them there.
left them there.
left them there.
leave them there.
Je-sus, dear Je-sus, Je-sus is my joy and song;
that bright throng.

Controlled by D. E. Dortch.

156. BY NO OTHER NAME.

W. HALPIN. D. E. DORTCH.

1. Come to Je - sus, dear sin - ner, He is wait-ing to save; He will
2. Come to Je - sus, dear sin - ner, And for-sake all your sin; Peace and
3. Come to Je - sus, dear sin - ner, Stand no lon-ger in doubt; Who-so-
4. Come to Je - sus, dear sin - ner, While 'tis yet called to-day; For the
wash you and cleanse you, In his blood's crimson wave; All the dark past will
com - fort he'll give you, If you let him come in; Tho' your sins be like
ev - er comes to him, He'll in no wise cast out; You may bring him your
mo-ments are pass-ing, Swift-ly pass-ing a-way; If the last chance is
van-ish, With its sin and its shame,
mountains, He can save you the same,
bur-den, That has brought you such blame,
slight-ed, O the an-guish and shame,
And sal-va-tion is giv - en, By
REFRAIN.
no oth - er name, By no oth - er name, By no oth - er name,
Our sal - va - tion is giv - en By no oth - er name.

Controlled by D. E. Dortch.

157. IN HIS NAME WE GO FORTH.

F. M. D. FRANK M. DAVIS.

Boldly.
1. In the name of Je - sus go we forth To wage a war with sin;
2. In the name of Je - sus go we forth His ban- ner to up-hold;
3. In the name of Je - sus go we forth A faith- ful hap- py throng,
By the pow'r and might of him we serve We shall the bat - tle win.
We are bat-tling for the cause of right And in that cause are bold.
In the cit - y of our Lord we'll join The grand tri-umph-ant song.
CHORUS.
In his name go we forth To
In his name go we forth
meet the might - y foe, March-ing close a - round the
might-y foe;
ban- ner of the cross, On to vic - to - ry we go.

158. THE KING WE OWN.

W. F. McC. W. F. McCAULEY.

1. On-ward is our war cry! Pass the word a-long, Bear our ban-ner brave-ly, Lift the vic-tor's song; Ma-ny mon-archs proud-ly Claim our be-ing's throne—Jesus, King of glo-ry, is the King we own.
2. Press we on to con-quer, Not with human might, Clad in God's own ar-mor, Sword of Spir-it bright. Cour-age! do not fal-ter, For his word hath shown We shall have the power of the King we own!
3. Soon the con-flict end-ed, More than conq'rors we, Glo-ry, praise, and hon-or To our Sav-iour be! Then we'll shout ho-san-na, And up-on his throne Reign in joy for-ev-er with the King we own!
CHORUS.
On-ward to the con-flict! Forward to the prize! Up-ward to the glo-ry shin-ing in the skies! Tear each i-dol rul-er

THE KING WE OWN. Concluded.

From God's temple down—Jesus King of glo-ry is the King we'll crown!

159. BATTLE HYMN.

ARR. BY MRS. G. K. LITTLE.

1. Am I a sol-dier of the cross, A foll-'wer of the Lamb, And shall I fear to own his cause, Or blush to speak his name?
2. Must I be car-ried to the skies On flow-'ry beds of ease, While oth-ers fought to win the prize And sailed through bloody seas?
3. Are there no foes for me to face? Must I not stem the flood? Is this vile world a friend to grace To help me on to God?
4. Sure I must fight if I would reign, Increase my courage, Lord; I'll bear the toil, endure the pain, Sup-port-ed by thy word.
CHORUS.
And when the battle's over
D. S.—And when the battle's o - ver
1
we shall wear a crown! yes, we shall wear a crown! yes, we shall wear a crown!
we shall wear a crown! (Omit 2d and last time.)
2
FINE.
D. S.
In the new Je-ru-sa-lem! Wear a crown! wear a crown!
Wear a crown! wear a crown!

160. WHERE THE LIVING WATERS FLOW.

R. KELSO CARTER. EDWARD E. NICKERSON.

1. Rest to the wea - ry soul And ach - ing breast is giv'n, Down where the
2. For thee, my soul, for thee These priceless joys were bought, Down where the
3. Come, with the ransom'd train, The Saviour's prais-es sing, Down where the
4. And soon, be-fore his face, We'll praise the Lord a-bove, Down where the
liv-ing waters flow; Grace makes the wounded whole, Love fills our hearts with heav'n,
liv-ing waters flow; Thine is the mer-cy free, That Christ to earth has brought,
liv-ing waters flow; Re-joice! the Lamb was slain, Adore! he reigns a king,
liv-ing waters flow; Tri-umphant thro' his grace, Made perfect by his love,
REFRAIN.
Down where the living waters flow. Down where the living waters flow, . . .
living waters flow,
Down where the tree of life doth grow, I'm liv - ing in the light, for
Je - sus and the right, Down where the liv - ing wa - ters flow.
liv - ing waters flow.

161. SUNSHINE AND SHADOW.

E. D. MUND. E. S. LORENZ.

1. When I walk'd with my Lord in the sun-shine, His com-panion-ship was sweet;
2. When I stood on the mount in the sun-shine, Felt I strong to walk a - lone;
3. When I walk'd with my Lord in the sunshine, With my love was mingled pride;
4. Oh, how precious the walk in the dark-ness! Oh how dear the hours of pain!
Then I wandered with him in the shad - ow, And my joy was made complete.
Then I groped in the gloom of the val - ley, And my helplessness was shown.
When the dark shadows fell I was hum-bled, And my love was pu - ri - fied.
When the Sav-iour is walk-ing be-side me, Mak-ing loss suprem-est gain.
CHORUS.
Ev - 'ry-where, dark or fair, Where my Sav-iour leads me will I
glad - ly go; Up on the mount-ain, down in the val - ley,
Ev - 'ry step he leads me rich - er grace doth show.

162. SAILOR ON THE OCEAN.

W. A. O. W. A. OGDEN.

1. Sail - or, on the o - cean sail - ing, sail - ing, See the bea- con
2. Pil - grim, on the high - way go - ing, go - ing, On thy jour-ney
3. Shepherd, who thy flock art guid-ing, guid-ing, Lead them in - to
light a - far; Bless- ed ones thy craft are hail - ing, hail - ing,
here be - low, There's a per- fect 'Guide' e'er show- ing, show-ing
pas- tures fair; By the bless- ed 'Rock' be hid - ing, hid - ing,
Yon-der from the har- bor bar.
Thee the way that thou should 'st go.
Where the cooling wa- ters are.
REFRAIN.
Sail - or, sail - or on life's o - cean,
Pil- grim, pil-grim on life's jour-ney,
Shepherd, shepherd gent - ly guid - ing,
Look to the 'Light' that's shin- ing clear; In the way of beau- ty,
Look to the 'Guide' he's ev - er near; In the way of beau- ty,
Look to the 'Rock,' it stand- eth near; In the way of beau- ty,
In the path of du - ty, Go thou and nev - er fear.

163. BOLDLY STAND FOR CHRIST.

F. M. D. FRANK M. DAVIS.

1. Bold-ly stand for Christ in the battle's strife, Let your courage e'er be shown;
2. Bold-ly stand for Christ whatso-e'er be- fall, All your pilgrim journey through;
3. Bold-ly stand for Christ till the bat-tle's o'er, Till the vic- to - ry is won;
Raise his standard high ov - er all the earth, Bold-ly stand for Christ a- lone.
Strive to en- ter in- to the promised rest, To the rest prepared for you.
Then how sweet the words of the Lord will be When he says to thee "Well done!"
CHORUS.
Bold- ly stand . . . . . for Christ a - lone, Who is
Bold - ly stand stand for Christ a- lone,
faith - - ful to his own; Raise his
Who is faith-ful faith - ful to his own;
standard high ov - er all the earth, Boldly stand for Christ a - lone.

164. THE UNCLOUDED DAY.

(May be used as a solo.)

Words and Melody by J. K. ALWOOD.

Arranged by J. F. KINSEY.

Moderato.

1. Oh, they tell me of a home far be-yond the skies, Oh, they tell me of a
2. Oh, they tell me of a home where my friends have gone, Oh, they tell me of that
3. Oh, they tell me of the King in his beau-ty there, And they tell me that mine
4. Oh, they tell me that he smiles on his chil-dren there, And his smiles drives their
home far a-way; Oh, they tell me of a home where no storm-clouds rise,
land far a-way; Where the tree of life in e-ter-nal bloom,
eyes shall be-hold; Where he sits on the throne that is whit-er than snow,
sorrows all a-way; And they tell me that no tears ev-er come a-gain,
Oh, they tell me of an un-cloud-ed day; Oh, the land of cloud-less
Sheds its fragrance thro' the un-cloud-ed day; Oh, the land of cloud-less
In the cit-y that is made of gold; Oh, that land mine eyes shall
In that love-ly land of un-cloud-ed day; Oh, that land of love-ly
day, Oh, the land of an un-cloud-ed sky; Oh, they tell me of a
day, Oh, the land of an un-cloud-ed sky; Oh, they tell me of my
see, Oh, that land of an un-cloud-ed sky; Oh, they tell me of the
smiles, Oh, the smiles of his love-beaming eye; Oh, the King in his

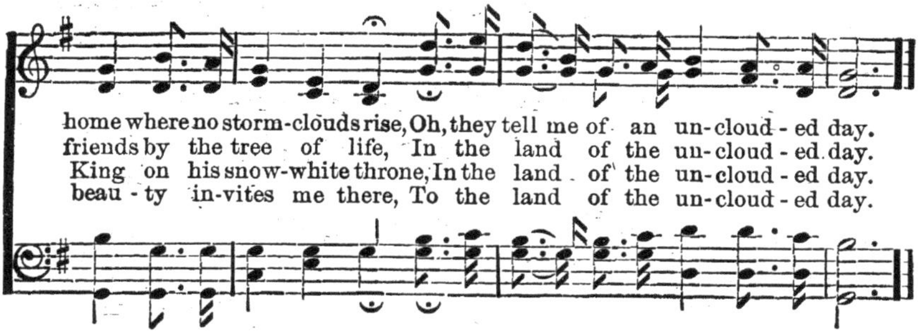
home where no storm-clouds rise, Oh, they tell me of an un-cloud-ed day.
friends by the tree of life, In the land of the un-cloud-ed day.
King on his snow-white throne, In the land of the un-cloud-ed day.
beau-ty in-vites me there, To the land of the un-cloud-ed day.

165. THE PRODIGAL SON.

J. J. MAXFIELD. LUCIUS LUTTRELL.

1. Far from home my feet are stray-ing, Shall I lon-ger roam?
2. Spent is all my boast-ed liv-ing, Fam-ine at the door!
3. Oth-er eyes for me are weeping, Child of ma-ny prayers;
4. I will go un-to my Fa-ther, Wretch-ed and un-done;
Fine.
Still my Fa-ther's voice is say-ing, Child come home, child come home.
What of sor-row's ghast-ly giv-ing Lack I more, lack I more.
I have sown and now am reap-ing On-ly tares, on-ly tares!
I would be a ser-vant rath-er Not a son, not a son.
D. S.—I may find a Fa-ther's bless-ing Wait-ing there, wait-ing there.
Chorus.
D. S.
I will go my sins con-fess-ing Bow-ing low in prayer;

Controlled by D. E. Dortch.

166. LET ME REST.

DR. H. BONAR. H. N. LINCOLN.

1. In the shad-ow of the Rock let me rest, ... When I
2. On the parch'd and des - ert way where I tread . . . . . With the
3. I in peace will rest me here till I see . . . . . . That the
let me rest,
feel the tem-pest's shock thrill my breast; All in
scorch-ing noon-tide ray o'er my head, Let me
skies a - gain are fair o - ver me; That the
thrill my breast;
vain the storm shall sweep while I hide, ...
find a wel - come shade cool and still, ...
burn-ing heats are past and the day . . . .
while I hide,
And my tran-quil vig - il keep by thy side.
And my wea - ry steps be stayed by thy will.
Bids the trav - el - er at last go his way.
by thy side,

By permission.

LET ME REST. Concluded.

CHORUS.
In the shad-ow of the Rock let me rest, In the
shad-ow of the Rock let me rest; When I feel the tem-pest's
shock thrill my breast, ... In the shadow of the Rock let me rest.
thrill my breast,

167. WILL YOU MEET US?

ANON. AMERICAN MELODY.

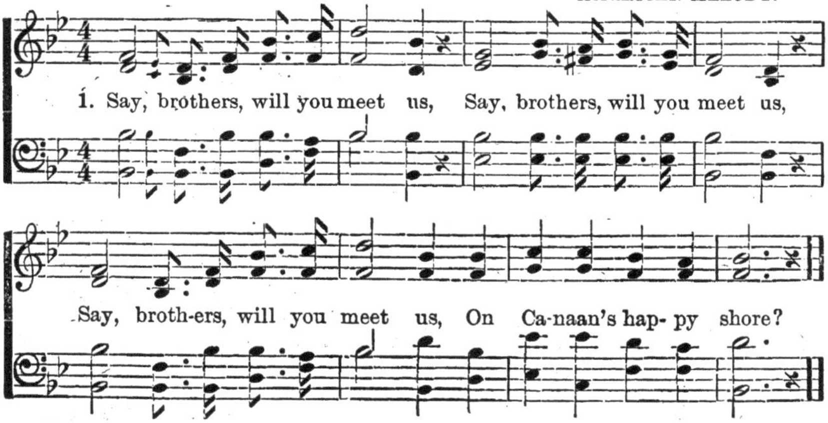
1. Say, brothers, will you meet us, Say, brothers, will you meet us,
Say, broth-ers, will you meet us, On Ca-naan's hap-py shore?

2 Say, sisters, will you meet us
On Canaan's happy shore?

3 By the grace of God I'll meet you
On Canaan's happy shore.

4 That will be a happy meeting
On Canaan's happy shore.

5 Jesus lives and reigns forever
On Canaan's happy shore.

168. AROUND THE SAVIOUR'S LOFTY THRONE.

THOMAS KELLY. J. H. RUEBUSH.

1. A-round the Saviour's loft - y throne Ten-thousand times ten-thousand sing;
2. Je - sus, thou ev - er - last- ing King, To thee the praise of heav'n belongs;
3. Tho' sin de - file our wor-ship here, We hope ere long thy face to view,
They wor-ship him as God a - lone, And crown him ev - er - last - ing King.
Yet smile on us who fain would bring The trib-ute of our hum-ble songs.
In heav'n with an - gels to ap- pear, And praise thy name as an-gels do.
CHORUS.
Let us join . . . . the an-gels' song, While they
Let us join the an-gels' song, Let us join the an-gels' song, While they
sing . . . . . . around the throne, And our cheer - ful
sing around the throne, While they sing around the throne, And our cheerful notes we'll raise
notes we'll raise In a grate- ful, grate-ful song of praise.
and our cheerful notes we'll raise,

169. THE TRIED AND TRUE.

E. D. MUND. E. S. LORENZ.

1. In the legion so brave is your name enrolled, The Tried and True!
2. O how bless-ed are they who have lost all fear! The Tried and True!
3. Dai-ly con-flicts will strengthen the steadfast heart, The Tried and True;
4. O-ver yon-der is gleaming the crown of life, Ye Tried and True!
Does the Lord know you well as a vet-'ran bold? Has he faith in you?
Who with faith all serene see the foe draw near They shall soon sub-due.
Ev-'ry vict'-ry will cour-age and faith im-part, Give new pow'r to do.
To the joy of that rest when ye end your strife, Christ will welcome you!
CHORUS.
Are you one of the Tried and True? Are you
Tried and True?
one of the Tried and True? In the bat-tle's
Tried and True?
din are you sure to win? Are you one of the Tried and True?

170. MY HEAVENLY HOME.

Respectfully inscribed to Hon. M. B. Templeton, of Waxahachie, Texas.

REV. W. H. BERRY. D. E. DORTCH.

1. There's a land where 'tis morn-ing for - ev - er, There no
2. There the riv - er of life, ev - er flow - ing, Keeps the
3. O how sweet when our war - fare is o - ver, And we
4. Sweet-er still it will be with our Sav - iour In that
clouds ev - er dark-en the sky; Those who meet in that land naught can
hills and the vales bright and fair; And the Sav - iour, his pres - ence be -
pass from the scene of earth's strife, It will be in that land to dis -
land of his glo - ry to meet, To re - joice in the light of his
sev - er, There true friend-ship and love nev - er die.
stow-ing, Fills with bliss ev - 'ry heart that is there.
cov - er Hearts we know to be true in this life.
fa - vor, With the glo - ri - fied saints at his feet.
CHORUS.
O that land is my home,
O that land, that beau-ti-ful land, is my home, my peaceful home! Oft in

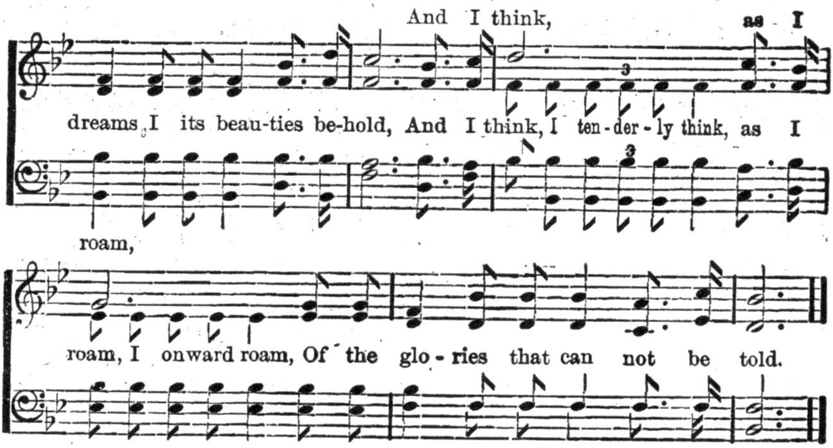
And I think, as I
dreams, I its beau-ties be-hold, And I think, I ten-der-ly think, as I
roam,
roam, I onward roam, Of the glo-ries that can not be told.

171. TRUSTING IN THEE.

W. F. McC. W. F. McCAULEY.

1. Sav-iour, I long to come, Yet fear to fall; Weak-ness a-lone am I, Sins dark en-thrall.
2. Could I the vict-'ry win, If I should try? Ma-ny the vows I've made, Brok-en they lie.
3. Wea-ry at heart I sink, Trust self no more: Je-sus, my all I yield, Thy grace im-plore.
REFRAIN.
1. 2. Yet I will trust in thee, Thou Lamb of Cal-va-ry; Thy blood can set me free, Trust-ing in thee.
3. Now I will trust in thee, Thou Lamb of Cal-va-ry; Thy blood will set me free, Trust-ing in thee.

172. RING, YE SWEET BELLS.

J. M. DUDLEY. SAM'L MITCHELL.

1. Glad - ly we hail the sweet mu - sic of bells; They are
2. Hush ye the clan - gor and tur - moil of life, Bid the
3. Ring, ye sweet bells, the e - van - gel di - vine; Fill the
ring-ing and peal - ing o - ver the land; Gent - ly the sound to de -
wea - ry re-joice,—to - day they may rest; Calm-ing life's fe - ver, sub-
earth with your mu - sic, soothe it with peace; Hearts that were bro-ken no
vo - tion com - pels, And in pres-ence di - vine we stand.
du - ing its strife, Her-ald wide - ly the Lord's day blest.
more may re - pine,—Now their sor - row and pain must cease.
CHORUS.
Ring, ye sweet bells! . . . . Hail the day of the Lord! . . . .
In-to our hearts . . . Ring the blessing of peace! . . . .
ring, ye sweet bells! hail the day of the Lord!
in-to our hearts ring the blessing of peace!
Ring, ye sweet bells! . . . . Join in grandest ac - cord! . . . .
ring, ye sweet bells! join in grandest accord!

2
Ring, ye sweet bells, ... May your chime never cease! . . . . .
ring, ye sweet bells,
may your chime never cease!

173. RING, YE BELLS.

REV. W. H. BERRY. D. E. DORTCH.

1. Ring, ye bells, in notes of glad-ness, Greet with joy the ris - ing morn;
2. See him laid with - in the man-ger, An - gel throngs his ad - vent sing;
3. Heav'n delight - ed bends a-bove him, Pour-ing mu - sic from the skies;
4. Hail thou long de-sired of na - tions, Prophet, Priest and King of men,
FINE.
Bid the world for-sake its sad - ness, Christ the Son of God is born.
Shepherds greet the glo - rious stranger, Wise men hail him as their King.
From the hearts on earth that love him, To high heav'n his prais - es rise.
Fill thy heav'n ap-point - ed sta - tions, Lead us back to God a - gain.
D. S.—Ring, ye bells, in notes of glad-ness, Greet with joy the ris - ing morn.
CHORUS.
D. S.
Ring, ye bells, ring, ye bells, Ring, ye bells, for Christ is born;

174. THE CHRISTMAS BELLS.

REV. I. BALTZELL. WINTON J. BALTZELL.

1st Div.
2d Div.
1. Ring out the sweet notes of the Christ - mas bells,
2. We're hap - py to - day as we list to the bells,
3. We'll ech - o the notes of re - joic - ing a - gain,
The Christ - mas bells, the Christ-mas bells; Ring out the sweet
The Christ - mas bells, the Christ-mas bells; We'll sing of re-
The Christ - mas bells, the Christ-mas bells; We'll sing with sweet
notes of the Christ - mas bells, This beau - ti - ful Christmas morn.
demption—sweet sto - ry to tell, This beau - ti - ful Christmas morn.
voic - es the gladsome re - frain, This beau - ti - ful Christmas morn.
With ju - bi - lant voic - es we'll mer - ri - ly sing
We'll tell of his mer - cy, we'll tell of his love,
Then ring out the notes of re - demp - tion once more,

THE CHRISTMAS BELLS. Concluded.

1st Div.
2d Div.
O ring the sweet bells, the Christ-mas bells, We'll glad - ly re -
While they ring the sweet bells, the Christ-mas bells, We'll car - ol with
With the Christ - mas bells, the Christ-mas bells, Let mu - sic go
mem-ber the heav - en-born King, This beau - ti - ful Christ-mas morn.
an - gel - ic harp-ers a - bove, This beau - ti - ful Christ-mas morn.
ring- ing from shore un - to shore, This beau - ti - ful Christ-mas morn.
Refrain.
O mer - ri - ly, mer - ri - ly sing the glad sto - ry That
Je - sus, our Sav- iour is born, Ring out the glad notes with the
Christ - mas bells, This beau - ti - ful Christ- mas morn.

175. THE STAR OF BETHLEHEM.

REV. J. H. MARTIN, D. D. E. S. LORENZ.

1. There is a star, ... of all most bright, ... That glitters
2. It tells us of . . . . a Saviour born, ... Me-mo-rial
3. It speaks to us . . . . . . of sins for-giv'n, ... Re-veals the
on . . . . the brow of night; A shin-ing orb . . . . . . the
of . . . . the hap - py morn When an-gels hast - - - 'ning
path . . . . to God and heav'n; It shines up-on . . . . . . our
love-liest, best, ... More clear and sweet than all the rest:
to the earth . . . . . . Proclaim the tid - ings of his birth:
dark-ened way . . . . And guides to realms of end - less day;
The fair - est, most at - tract - ive gem, The pleas-ing Star of
Pre-pared with roy - al di - a - dem To crown the Babe of
Fair, love - ly, bright and beau-teous gem, The ra - diant Star of

STAR OF BETHLEHEM. Concluded.

Beth - le - hem, The fair - est, most (the fair - est, most at - tract-ive
Beth - le - hem, Prepared with roy- (prepared with roy - al dia - a-
Beth - le - hem, Fair, love-ly, bright (fair, love - ly, bright and beauteous
gem), at - tract-ive gem, The pleas-ing Star of Beth - le - hem,
dem), al di - a - dem, To crown the Babe of Beth - le - hem,
gem), and beauteous gem, The ra-diant Star of Beth - le - hem,
The fair - est, most (the fair - est, most at - tract - ive
Prepared with roy- (pre - pared with roy - al di - a-
Fair, love - ly, bright,(fair, love - ly, bright and beauteous
gem), at - tract - ive gem, The pleas-ing Star of Beth - le - hem.
dem), al dia - a - dem, To crown the Babe of Beth - le - hem.
gem), and beauteous gem, The ra-diant Star of Beth - le - hem.

176. EASTER BELLS.

C. H. G. CHAS. H. GABRIEL.

1. Ring out, oh, hap - py Eas - ter bells, Fill earth and air with
2. Ring out, oh, hap - py Eas - ter bells, Your cheer-ful voice of
3. Ring out, oh, hap - py Eas - ter bells, To all the world your
nois - y swells, And ma - ny tune - ful lay; A - far and near let
joy im - pels The hu - man heart to praise; Your mer - ry rhyme of
mu - sic tells Of fair - er things a - bove; Our songs of joy we
songs of cheer, In car - ols sweet the joy re - peat Of res - ur - rec - tion day.
clang and chime, With ho - ly fire our souls in - spire, A sac - ri - fice to raise.
will employ, To praise his name and wide proclaim The wonders of his love.
CHORUS.
Ring, sweet bells, Oh, Eas - ter bells, Oh, hap - py bells,
Ring, sweet bells, sweet Easter bells, Oh, ring, sweet bells,
Then ring, sweet bells,
Then ring, sweet bells, sweet Eas - ter bells, Ring out, oh, hap - pv bells.

177. SWEET HALLELUJAHS.

REV. EDWIN PAXTON HOOD. E. S. L.

1. Sweet hal-le-lu-jahs! the birds and the blossoms Chant forth in har-mo-ny praise to the Lord: Sweet hal-le-lu-jahs from pen-i-tent bo-soms; Angels in rap-ture re-ech-o the word.
2. Sweet hal-le-lu-jahs! the works of cre-a-tion Praise him who on-ly may e'er be a-dored: Sweet-er the thrill of a new an-i-ma-tion, When sin-ners, pardoned, sing praise to the Lord.
3. Sweet hal-le-lu-jahs! the great congre-ga-tion Round the white throne shall re-ech-o the word; Pass with their palms thro' the gates of sal-va-tion, Sing-ing for-ev-er their praise to the Lord.
CHORUS.
Sweet hal-le-lu-jahs!
ECHO.
Sweet hal-le-lu-jahs! Hear the hap-py song as it floats on the air!
ECHO.
Sweet hal-le-lu-jahs! Sweet hallelujahs! Praise divine is ring-ing ev-'ry-where.

178. IN BLOSSOM TIME.

E. D. MUND. E. S. L.

1. The win-ter reigns no more, But field and for-est o'er The blos-som
2. The world to joy a-wakes, The win-ter's si-lence breaks And laughs with
3. While all the world is gay Shall hearts be cold and gray? No! we will
time re-joic-es; While ev-'ry tree-clad hill, And laughing, rippling rill,
joy so mer-ry; The bees that skim the air To buds and blossoms fair
join the cho-rus! Thro' all the sum-mer days We'll sing God's cheerful praise,
Its full de-light now voic-es. The birds sing hap-py tunes the
The hap-py mu-sic car-ry. Thro' all his course a-cross the
Who doth Spring's joy re-store us. With cheer-ful hearts and mer-ry
Duet.
whole day long, The woods are ring-ing with their glad-some song:
heav-ens blue, The sun re-joic-es in his pow'r a-new:
voic-es sweet His mer-cies ten-der we will oft re-peat:
Chorus.
For it is hap-py blos-som time! De-light-ful blos-som time!

179

FROM every stormy wind that blows,
From every swelling tide of woes,
There is a calm, a sure, retreat;
'Tis found before the mercy-seat.

There is a place where Jesus sheds
The oil of gladness on our heads,—
A place of all on earth most sweet;
It is the blood-bought mercy-seat.

There is a scene where spirits blend,
Where friend holds fellowship with friend;
Though sundered far, by faith they meet
Around one common mercy-seat.

There, there, on eagle wings we soar,
And sin and sense molest no more;
And heaven comes down our souls to greet,
And glory crowns the mercy-seat.

180

WE praise thee, O God, for the Son of thy love,
For Jesus, who died and is now gone above.

Cho.—Hallelujah! thine the glory;
Hallelujah! Amen;
Hallelujah! thine the glory;
Revive us again.

All glory and praise to the Lamb that was slain,
Who has borne all our sins, and has cleansed every stain.

Revive us again; fill each heart with thy love;
May each soul be rekindled with fire from above.

181

THE great Physician now is near,
The sympathizing Jesus;
He speaks, the drooping heart to cheer;
Oh, hear the voice of Jesus.

Cho.—Sweetest note in seraph song,
Sweetest name on mortal tongue,
Sweetest carol ever sung,—
Jesus, blessed Jesus.

Your many sins are all forgiven,—
Oh, hear the voice of Jesus;
Go on your way in peace to heaven,
And wear a crown with Jesus.

All glory to the dying Lamb!
I now believe in Jesus;
I love the blessed Savior's name,
I love the name of Jesus.

182

I HEAR the Savior say,
"Thy strength indeed is small;
Child of weakness, watch and pray,
Find in me thine all in all."

Cho.—Jesus paid it all,
All to him I owe:
Sin had left a crimson stain;
He washed it white as snow.

For nothing good have I
Whereby his grace to claim,—
I'll wash my garments white
In the blood of Calvary's Lamb.

When from my dying bed
My ransomed soul shall rise,
Then "Jesus paid it all"
Shall rend the vaulted skies.

183

JOY to the world! the Lord is come!
Let earth receive her King;
Let every heart prepare him room,
And heaven and nature sing.

Joy to the earth! the Savior reigns!
Let men their songs employ,
While fields and floods, rocks, hills, and plains,
Repeat the sounding joy.

No more let sin and sorrow grow
Nor thorns infest the ground;
He comes to make his blessings flow
Far as the curse is found.

He rules the world with truth and grace,
And makes the nations prove
The glories of his righteousness
And wonders of his love.

184

BLOW ye the trumpet, blow!
The gladly solemn sound
Let all the nations know,
To earth's remotest bound.
The year of jubilee is come;
Return, ye ransomed sinners, home.

Jesus, our great High Priest,
Has full atonement made.
Ye weary spirits, rest;
Ye mourning souls, be glad.
The year of jubilee is come;
Return, ye ransomed sinners, home.

Exalt the Lamb of God,
The sin-atoning Lamb;
Redemption by his blood
Through all the world proclaim.
The year of jubilee is come;
Return, ye ransomed sinners, home.

185

COME, every soul by sin oppressed,
There's mercy with the Lord,
And he will surely give you rest
By trusting in his word.

Cho.—Only trust him, only trust him,
Only trust him now;
He will save you, he will save you
He will save you now.

For Jesus shed his precious blood
Rich blessings to bestow;
Plunge now into the crimson flood
That washes white as snow.

Yes, Jesus is the Truth, the Way
That leads you into rest;
Believe in him without delay,
And you are fully blest.

186

BLEST be the tie that binds
  Our hearts in Christian love;
The fellowship of kindred minds
  Is like to that above.

Before our Father's throne
  We pour our ardent prayers;
Our fears, our hopes, our aims, are one
  Our comforts and our cares.

We share our mutual woes,
  Our mutual burdens bear;
And often for each other flows
  The sympathizing tear.

187

OH, for a closer walk with God,
  A calm and heavenly frame,
A light to shine upon the road
  That leads me to the Lamb.

Return, O holy Dove, return,
  Sweet messenger of rest;
I hate the sins that made thee mourn,
  And drove thee from my breast.

The dearest idol I have known,
  Whate'er that idol be,
Help me to tear it from thy throne,
  And worship only thee.

188

A CHARGE to keep I have,
  A God to glorify,
A never-dying soul to save
  And fit it for the sky.

Arm me with jealous care,
  As in thy sight to live;
And, oh, thy servant, Lord, prepare
  A strict account to give.

Help me to watch and pray
  And on thyself rely,
Assured, if I my trust betray,
  I shall forever die.

189

THE holiest place stands open wide;
  Enter by the blood of Jesus!
The shadowing veil now hangs aside;
  Enter by the blood of Jesus!

CHO.—Within the sacred veil
  Pure love and peace prevail,
  God's promise ne'er can fail;
  Enter by the blood of Jesus!

Come enter now this holiest place;
  Enter by the blood of Jesus!
Where Christ unveils his shining face;
  Enter by the blood of Jesus!

Here, soul, is cleansing, full and free;
  Enter by the blood of Jesus!
Here God's Shekinah you can see;
  Enter by the blood of Jesus!

By faith your soul may now prevail;
  Enter by the blood of Jesus!
And pass beyond the second veil;
  Enter by the blood of Jesus!

190

I AM coming to the cross;
  I am poor and weak and blind;
I am counting all but dross;
  I shall full salvation find.

CHO.—I am trusting, Lord, in thee,
  Blest Lamb of Calvary;
  Humbly at thy cross I bow;
  Save me, Jesus, save me now.

Long my heart has sighed for thee;
  Long has evil reigned within.
Jesus sweetly speaks to me,
  "I will cleanse you from all sin."

Here I give my all to thee,
  Friends and time and earthly store
Soul and body, thine to be,—
  Wholly thine for evermore.

In thy promises I trust;
  Now I feel thy blood applied;
I am prostrate in the dust,
  I with Christ am crucified.

191

JUST as I am, without one plea
  But that thy blood was shed for me,
And that thou bid'st me come to thee,
  O Lamb of God! I come, I come.

Just as I am, and waiting not
To rid my soul of one dark blot,
To thee, whose blood can cleanse each spot,
  O Lamb of God! I come, I come.

Just as I am, though tossed about
With many a conflict, many a doubt,
Fightings within and fears without,
  O Lamb of God! I come, I come.

Just as I am, poor, wretched, blind,—
Sight, riches, healing of the mind,
Yea, all I need, in thee to find,—
  O Lamb of God! I come, I come.

192

COME, we that love the Lord,
  And let our joys be known;
Join in a song with sweet accord,
  And thus surround the throne.

CHO.—We're marching to Zion,
  Beautiful, beautiful Zion;
  We're marching upward to Zion,
  The beautiful city of God.

Let those refuse to sing
  Who never knew our God;
But children of the heavenly King
  May speak their joys abroad.

The hill of Zion yields
  A thousand sacred sweets
Before we reach the heavenly fields
  Or walk the golden streets.

Then let our songs abound,
  And every tear be dry;
We're marching through Immanuel's ground
  To fairer worlds on high.

193

COME to Jesus.
2 He will save you.
3 Oh, believe him.
4 He is able.
5 He is willing.
6 He'll receive you.
7 Call upon him.
8 He will hear you.
9 Look unto him.
10 He'll forgive you.
11 Flee to Jesus.
12 He will cleanse you.
13 He will clothe you.
14 Jesus loves you.
15 Don't reject him.
16 Only trust him.
17 Hallelujah, Amen.

194

JESUS, lover of my soul,
Let me to thy bosom fly,
While the nearer waters roll,
While the tempest still is high.
Hide me, O my Savior, hide,
Till the storm of life is past;
Safe into the haven guide,—
Oh, receive my soul at last.

Other refuge have I none;
Hangs my helpless soul on thee;
Leave, oh, leave me not alone;
Still support and comfort me.
All my trust on thee is stayed;
All my help from thee I bring;
Cover my defenseless head
With the shadow of thy wing.

195

OH, happy day that fixed my choice
On thee, my Savior and my God;
Well may this glowing heart rejoice,
And tell its raptures all abroad.

CHO.— Happy day! happy day!
When Jesus washed my sins away.
He taught me how to watch and pray,
And live rejoicing every day.
Happy day! happy day!
When Jesus washed my sins away.

'Tis done,—the great transaction's done;
I am my Lord's, and he is mine;
He drew me, and I followed on,
Rejoiced to own the call divine.

Now rest, my long divided heart,—
Fixed on this blissful center, rest;
Here I have found a nobler part,
Here heavenly pleasures fill my breast.

196

SWEET hour of prayer! sweet hour of prayer,
That calls me from a world of care,
And bids me at my Father's throne,
Make all my wants and wishes known.
In seasons of distress and grief
My soul has often found relief,
And oft escaped the tempter's snare,
By thy return, sweet hour of prayer.

Sweet hour of prayer! sweet hour of prayer!
Thy wings shall my petitions bear
To him whose truth and faithfulness
Engage the waiting soul to bless;
And since he bids me seek his face,
Believe his word, and trust his grace,
I'll cast on him my every care,
And wait for thee, sweet hour of prayer.

197

MORE love to thee, O Christ!
More love to thee!
Hear thou the prayer I make
On bended knee;
This is my earnest plea,—
More love, O Christ, to thee,
More love to thee!

Once earthly joy I craved,
Sought peace and rest;
Now thee alone I seek,—
Give what is best:
This all my prayer shall be,—
More love, O Christ, to thee,
More love to thee.

198

WHAT a friend we have in Jesus,
All our sins and griefs to bear;
What a privilege to carry
Everything to God in prayer.
Oh, what peace we often forfeit,
Oh, what needless pain we bear,—
All because we do not carry
Everything to God in prayer.

Have we trials and temptations?
Is there trouble anywhere?
We should never be discouraged;
Take it to the Lord in prayer.
Can we find a friend so faithful,
Who will all our sorrows share?
Jesus knows our every weakness;
Take it to the Lord in prayer.

Are we weak and heavy laden,
Cumbered with a load of care?
Precious Savior, still our refuge,—
Take it to the Lord in prayer.
Do thy friends despise, forsake thee?
Take it to the Lord in prayer.
In his arms he'll take and shield thee;
Thou wilt find a solace there.

199

HE leadeth me—oh, blessed thought;
Oh, words with heav'nly comfort fraught,—
Whate'er I do, where'er I be,
Still 'tis God's hand that leadeth me.

REF.—He leadeth me, he leadeth me!
By his own hand he leadeth me;
His faithful follower I would be,
For by his hand he leadeth me.

Sometimes 'mid scenes of deepest gloom,
Sometimes where Eden's bowers bloom,
By waters still, o'er troubled sea,—
Still 'tis his hand that leadeth me.

Lord, I would clasp thy hand in mine,
Nor ever murmur nor repine,—
Content whatever lot I see,
Since 'tis my God that leadeth me.

200

FATHER, I stretch my hands to thee;
No other help I know;
If thou withdraw thyself from me,
Ah, whither shall I go?

CHO.—I do believe, I now believe,
That Jesus died for me,
And thro' his blood, his precious blood,
I shall from sin be free.

What did thine only Son endure
Before I drew my breath!
What pain, what labor, to secure
My soul from endless death!

Author of faith, to thee I lift
My weary, longing eyes;
Oh, may I now receive that gift;
My soul without it dies.

201

COME, thou Fount of every blessing,
Tune my heart to sing thy grace;
Streams of mercy, never ceasing,
Call for songs of loudest praise.
Teach me some melodious sonnet,
Sung by flaming tongues above;
Praise the mount,—I'm fixed upon it,—
Mount of thy redeeming love.

Here I'll raise my Ebenezer,
Hither by thy help I'm come;
And I hope by thy good pleasure
Safely to arrive at home.
Jesus sought me when a stranger,
Wand'ring from the fold of God;
He, to rescue me from danger,
Interposed his precious blood.

Oh, to grace how great a debtor
Daily I'm constrained to be!
Let thy goodness, like a fetter,
Bind my wand'ring heart to thee.
Prone to wander, Lord, I feel it,—
Prone to leave the God I love;
Here's my heart,—oh, take and seal it,—
Seal it for thy courts above.

202

NEARER, my God, to thee,
Nearer to thee!
E'en though it be a cross
That raiseth me,
Still all my song shall be,
Nearer, my God, to thee,
Nearer to thee!

Though, like the wanderer,
The sun gone down,
Darkness be over me,
My rest a stone,
Yet in my dreams I'd be
Nearer, my God, to thee,
Nearer to thee!

There let the way appear
Steps unto heaven;
All that thou sendest me
In mercy given;
Angels to beckon me
Nearer, my God, to thee,
Nearer to thee!

203

BEHOLD a Stranger at the door!
He gently knocks, has knocked before,
Has waited long, is waiting still;
You treat no other friend so ill.

CHO.—Oh, let the dear Savior come in,—
He'll cleanse thy heart from sin;
Oh, keep him no more out at the door,
But let the dear Savior come in.

Oh, lovely attitude! he stands
With melting heart and loaded hands;
Oh, matchless kindness! and he shows
This matchless kindness to his foes.

But will he prove a friend indeed?
He will,—the very Friend you need;
The Friend of sinners—yes, 'tis he,
With garments dyed on Calvary.

Rise, touched with gratitude divine,
Turn out his enemy and thine,—
That soul-destroying monster, sin,—
And let the heavenly Stranger in.

204

ALAS, and did my Savior bleed?
And did my Sov'reign die?
Would he devote that sacred head
For such a worm as I?

CHO.—Help me, dear Savior, thee to own,
And ever faithful be;
And when thou sittest on thy throne,
O Lord, remember me.

Was it for crimes that I have done
He groaned upon the tree?
Amazing pity! grace unknown!
And love beyond degree!

Well might I hide my blushing face.
While his dear cross appears,
Dissolve my heart in thankfulness,
And melt mine eyes to tears.

But drops of grief can ne'er repay
The debt of love I owe;
Here, Lord, I give myself away;
'Tis all that I can do.

205

OH, think of the home over there,
By the side of the river of light,
Where the saints, all immortal and fair,
Are robed in their garments of white.

REF.—Over there, over there,
Oh, think of the home over there.

Oh, think of the friends over there,
Who before us the journey have trod,
Of the songs that they breathe on the air
In their home in the palace of God.
REF.—Over there, over there,
Oh, think of the friends over there.

My Savior is now over there;
There my kindred and friends are at rest.
Then away from my sorrow and care
Let me fly to the land of the blest.
REF.—Over there, over there,
My Savior is now over there.

206

MY hope is built on nothing less
Than Jesus' blood and righteousness;
I dare not trust the sweetest frame,
But wholly lean on Jesus' name.

CHORUS.

On Christ, the Solid Rock, I stand;
‖: All other ground is sinking sand. :‖

When darkness seems to veil his face,
I rest on his unchanging grace;
In every high and stormy gale
My anchor holds within the veil.

His oath, his covenant, and blood
Support me in the whelming flood;
When all around my soul gives way,
He then is all my hope and stay.

207

THERE is a fountain filled with blood,
Drawn from Immanuel's veins,
And sinners plunged beneath that flood
Lose all their guilty stains.

CHO.—O glorious fountain!
Here will I stay,
And in thee ever
Wash my sins away.

The dying thief rejoiced to see
That fountain in his day,
And there may I, though vile as he,
Wash all my sins away.

Thou dying Lamb, thy precious blood
Shall never lose its power,
Till all the ransomed church of God
Are saved to sin no more.

208

MY Father is rich in houses and lands,
He holdeth the wealth of the world in his hands!
Of rubies and diamonds, of silver and gold,
His coffers are full; he has riches untold.

CHO.—I'm the child of a King,
The child of a King;
With Jesus, my Savior,
I'm the child of a King.

My Father's own Son, the Savior so fair,
Once wandered on earth human sorrow to share:
But now he is reigning forever on high;
He'll give us a home in the sweet by and by.

I once was an outcast stranger on earth,
A sinner by choice and an "alien" by birth;
But I've been "adopted"; my name's written down
An heir to a mansion, a robe, and a crown.

A tent or a cottage, why should I care?
They're building a palace for me over there!
Though exiled from home, yet my glad heart can sing,
All glory to God, I'm the child of a King.

209

ASLEEP in Jesus! blessed sleep,
From which none ever wake to weep;
A calm and undisturbed repose,
Unbroken by the dread of foes.

Asleep in Jesus! peaceful rest,
Whose waking is supremely blest;
No fear, no woes, shall dim the hour
Which manifests the Savior's power.

Asleep in Jesus! oh, for me
May such a blissful refuge be;
Securely shall my ashes lie,
And wait the summons from on high.

210

COME, ye sinners, poor and needy,
Weak and wounded, sick and sore;
Jesus ready stands to save you,
Full of pity, love, and pow'r.

Now, ye needy, come, and welcome;
God's free bounty glorify,
True belief and true repentance,
Every grace that brings you nigh.

Let not conscience make you linger,
Nor of fitness fondly dream;
All the fitness he requireth
Is to feel your need of him!

These words can be used with this chorus:

CHO.—Turn to the Lord and seek salvation,
Sound the praise of his near name;
Glory, honor, and salvation,
Christ, the Lord, is come to reign.

Or with the following:

CHO.—I will arise and go to Jesus,
He will embrace me in his arms;
In the arms of my dear Jesus,
Oh, there are ten thousand charms.

211

LORD, I care not for riches,
Neither silver nor gold;
I would make sure of heaven,
I would enter the fold.
In the book of thy kingdom,
With its pages so fair,
Tell me, Jesus, my Savior,
Is my name written there?

CHO.—Is my name written there,—
On the page white and fair?
In the book of thy kingdom,
Is my name written there?

Lord, my sins, they are many,
Like the sands of the sea,
But thy blood, O my Savior,
Is sufficient for me;
For thy promise is written
In bright letters that glow:
"Though your sins be as scarlet,
I will make them like snow."

Oh, that beautiful city,
With its mansions of light,
With its glorified beings,
In pure garments of white;
Where no evil thing cometh
To despoil what is fair;
Where the angels are watching,—
Yes, my name's written there.

INDEX.

Titles in small capitals. First lines in roman.

A beautiful story in God's book is told 95
A charge to keep I have 188
A Cup of Water 46
A Soldier of the Cross 75
Alas, and did my Savior bleed 204
All day long I'd bear the cross for 76
All for Jesus 76
All hail the power of Jesus' name 37
All praise to him who reigns above 20
Am I a soldier of the cross 75
Am I a soldier of the cross (chorus) 159
Amid the trials which I meet 61
Are You Counting the Cost 108
Are You for Jesus 36
Are You Ready for Service 94
Are you seeking for the truth 126
Around the Savior's Lofty Throne 168
Art thou burdened with thy sin 47
As you strive for the world 108
Asleep in Jesus 209
At the wondrous temple 62
Battle Hymn 159
Behold, a stranger at the door 203
Benediction 137
Beyond this life of hope and fears 70
Blessed be the Name 20
Blest be the tie that binds 186
Blow ye the trumpet 184
Boldly Stand for Christ 163
Brightly beams thy love, Lord Jesus. 5
Building on the Rock 63
By no Other Name 156
By the grace of God renewed 42
Call Them In 14
Cast Your Bread 98
Children of the Heavenly King 127
Christ Assures Us 84
Closer Than a Brother 147
Come drink of life's crystal fountain. 23
Come, every soul by sin oppressed 185
Come, Holy Spirit, Heavenly Dove 153
Come Sing to Me of Jesus' Love 38
Come, thou Fount of every blessing 201
Come to Jesus 193
Come to Jesus, dear sinner 156
Come to the Waters 80
Come Unto Me 139
Come, we that love the Lord 192
Come, ye sinners, poor 210
Coronation 37
Day by Day 42
Do It Now 73
Drink and Live 23
Easter Bells 176
Enough for Me 113
Enter the Pearly Gates 114
Exalt the Name of Jesus 131
Faith is mighty 67
Far from home my feet are straying 165
Father, I stretch my hands to thee 200
Fearing no Danger 71
Fill with lofty praise 90
For Christ and the Church 41
From every stormy wind that blows 179
From Jerusalem to Jericho 12
Gather flowers from the meadow 17
Give, Freely Give 143
Give, says the earth 143
Gladly we hail the sweet music of 172
Go Ye Into All the World 106
God Be With You 140
God Speed Them On 99
God's Flowers 17
Grace and Glory 134
Growing in Grace 101
Hail Ye the King 89
Hark to the words that once 114
Harvest Praise 154
He leadeth me 199
Hear the Savior Calling 52
Help me, Savior, more each day 101
His Leading Hand 129
Holy Spirit, Faithful Guide 13
Hosanna to Jesus 100
How do little birdies grow 124
How I Love Jesus 91
How oft this heart of mine 129
How our hearts will throb with 148
How You Grow 124
I am coming to the cross 190
I am nearing the port 79
I am Resting in the Savior's Love 60
I am safe in the Rock 123
I am Sheltered in Thee 123
I am the Way 22
I am trusting thee, dear Savior 51
I am waiting for the Master 24
I am walking with the Savior 138
I have found redemption in the 7
I hear a song, a song so sweet 133
I hear the Savior say 182
I wandered once in woe and shame 1
I was once in sin and far from God 77
I was once in sin and the darkness 92
I Will Come to Thee 35
I will sing all day 115
If 'tis but a cup of water 46
If you have a kind word, say it 73
I'll Live for Him 97
I'm waiting in the borderland 54
In Blossom Time 178
In from the highways 22
In His Name Go We Forth 157
In Newness of Life 66
In our grand Epworth League we are 96
In the Glad New Time 150
In the legion so brave is your name 169
In the name of Jesus go we forth 157
In the shadow of the Rock let me rest 166
Is the Spirit of God leading you 16
It Doth Not Yet Appear 34
It is Finished 74
It Redeemed Me 92
Jesus, I own thy pardon 141
Jesus is My Joy and Song 135
Jesus is the Blessed Name 33
Jesus is Waiting 65
Jesus, lover of my soul 194
Jesus, Savior, Pilot Me 145
Jesus Will Forgive 47
Join the Song 28
Joy to the world! the Lord 183
Just as I am 191
Just Beyond the River 117
Laban, S. M 45
Leaning on the Everlasting Arms 110

LEARN OF JESUS ... 126
LESSON FOR ETERNITY ... 109
LET ME REST ... 166
Let the light of life now shine ... 146
Let us join the happy song ... 28
LET US PAY OUR VOWS ... 130
LET YOUR LIGHT SO SHINE ... 32
LIFE AND LIGHT ... 111
LIGHT AND DARKNESS ... 119
Lights in the upper dwelling ... 119
LINGER NOT ... 142
LOOK UP, LIFT UP ... 96
LOOKOUT SONG ... 125
Lord, I care not for ... 211
LORD, I HAVE MADE THY WORD MY ... 93
LOVE IS KING ... 67
MAKE IT A FULL SALVATION ... 141
May the love of God be with you ... 49
More love to thee, O Christ ... 197
MUST I GO WITH EMPTY HANDS? ... 29
My faith looks up to thee ... 81
My Father is rich ... 208
My heart has a burden of joy to-day ... 132
MY HEAVENLY HOME ... 170
My hope is built on nothing less ... 206
My life, my love, I give to thee ... 97
My light and strength ... 134
My soul, be on thy guard ... 45
My soul is joyful in the Lord ... 111
Nearer, my God, to thee ... 202
NEARING THE PORT ... 79
NEW HAVEN ... 81
No one hath told me what this life ... 84
Not that we loved God ... 11
Often in our journey here ... 147
Oh, for a closer walk with God ... 187
Oh, happy day that fixed my choice ... 195
Oh, hast thou not heard of the ... 30
Oh, love surpassing knowledge ... 113
Oh, my heart is thrilled with ... 60
OH, THE JOY I FEEL ... 115
Oh, the peace that fills my soul ... 103
Oh, they tell me of a home ... 164
Oh, think of the home over there ... 205
Oh, what a lesson we all may learn ... 109
Oh, why do you wait ... 6
On sin's dark mountain ... 155
On the solid rock I am building ... 63
One name shall echo through the ... 27
Onward is our war cry ... 158
Open are the arms of Jesus ... 48
OPEN ARMS OF JESUS ... 48
Open your heart to the Spirit's ... 3
OVER JORDAN WE SHALL MEET ... 44
OVER THE WORLD ... 146
PASS UNDER THE ROD ... 15
PEACE, BE STILL ... 102
PRAISE ... 87
PRAISE HIM EVER ... 19
PRAISE THE LORD ... 9
Praise to the Father ... 87
Precious words I love to hear ... 120
QUICKLY COME ... 25
READY FOR THE MASTER ... 132
REDEEMING LOVE ... 83
REMEMBER ME ... 59
Rest to the weary soul ... 160
Ring out, O happy Easter bells ... 176
Ring out the sweet notes of the ... 174
RING, YE BELLS ... 173
RING, YE SWEET BELLS ... 172
ROCK OF AGES ... 57
SAIL ON ... 78
SAILOR ON THE OCEAN ... 162
SALVATION IS FREE ... 85
SATISFIED WITH JESUS ... 138
SAVED BY FAITH ... 7
SAVIOR, I COME ... 116
Savior, I long to come ... 171
Savior, in the morning I will come ... 35
Say, brothers, will you meet us ... 167
See, the morn is bright'ning ... 121
SENTENCE ... 11
Set the watch; trim the lamps ... 32
Should the "Forward, march," be ... 94
SHOULDER TO SHOULDER ... 128
SING HALLELUJAH ... 1
Sirs, what must I do to be saved ... 86
SITTING AT THE FEET OF JESUS ... 103
SOFTLY FADES THE TWILIGHT RAY ... 105
SOME DAY ... 133
Songs of adoration raise ... 19
SOW THE GOOD SEED ... 149
SOWING, EVER SOWING ... 56
SOWING IN TEARS ... 10
SOWING THE TARES ... 50
SOWING TIME ... 121
STAND THEREFORE ... 112
STEP IN THE LIFE-BOAT ... 68
SUN OF MY SOUL ... 151
SUNSHINE AND SHADOW ... 161
SUNSHINE IN THE SOUL ... 18
Sweet are the promises ... 104
SWEET HALLELUJAHS ... 177
Sweet hour of prayer ... 196
Sweetly the Savior's voice ... 139
TARRY WITH US ... 152
Tell it abroad till the world shall ... 72
TELL IT ALL TO JESUS ... 135
THE BLESSED BIBLE ... 58
THE CHRISTMAS BELLS ... 174
THE COMING OF THE LORD DRAWETH ... 21
THE DAY OF DAYS ... 90
THE EDEN LAND ... 31
THE FIELD OF THE MASTER ... 4
THE FRUITS OF THE SPIRIT ... 8
THE GLAD HEREAFTER ... 118
THE GOOD SAMARITAN ... 12
THE GRACE OF GOD ... 30
The grace of our Lord Jesus Christ ... 137
The great Physician now is near ... 181
THE HARBOR IN SIGHT ... 64
The holiest place stands open wide ... 189
THE KING WE OWN ... 158
The life-boat is launched on the wild ... 68
THE LOVE OF JESUS ... 5
THE MASTER WELCOMES THE ... 95
THE PRECIOUS NAME ... 27
THE PRODIGAL SON ... 165
THE SPIRIT OF CHRIST ... 2
THE SPIRIT OF GOD ... 16
THE STAR OF BETHLEHEM ... 175
THE TEMPLE OF PRAYER ... 62
THE TRIED AND TRUE ... 169
THE UNCLOUDED DAY ... 164
The waves roll high, the clouds are ... 78
The winter reigns no more ... 178
THE WONDROUS NAME ... 107
There are coming changes great ... 150
There are mansions for the blest ... 26
There is a cleansing, healing tide ... 25
There is a friend, a friend in need ... 88
There is a fountain filled ... 207
There is a name I love to hear ... 91
There is a name so sweet to me ... 33
There is a star of all most bright ... 175
THERE IS MUSIC IN MY SOUL ... 77
THERE IS NO FRIEND LIKE JESUS ... 88
There will be a fairer dawning ... 55
There's a city bright and fair ... 117
There's a dark, turbid stream ... 82
There's a fountain free flowing ... 122
There's a land where 'tis morning ... 170
THERE'S A LIGHT AT THE RIVER ... 82
There's a love that's begotten within ... 8
There's an Eden land o'er the ... 31
There's sunshine in my soul to-day ... 18
They go to preach the blessed word ... 99
They tell us the fields are ready ... 125
THOU THINKEST, LORD, OF ME ... 61

TILL WE MEET AGAIN ... 49
'Tis a lamp unto my feet ... 58
To the field of the Master ... 4
TRUSTING IN THEE ... 171
TRUSTING ONLY THEE ... 51
Turn thy steps from earth's ... 53
WAITING AT THE PORTAL ... 24
WAITING IN THE BORDERLAND ... 54
Wake the voice of gladness ... 154
WALK WITH THE SAVIOR ... 136
Walking with Jesus in newness of life 66
Wand'ring and weary, oh, why dost.. 65
WE ARE READY ... 144
We are sowing, ever sowing ... 56
We have entered royal service ... 130
We have heard a name of power ... 107
We praise thee, O God ... 180
WE SHALL REST AT THE FOUNTAIN ... 122
Weary with want and sin ... 116
WELCOME THE SPIRIT IN ... 3
WE'LL FOLLOW HIM ... 53
We're a happy pilgrim band ... 144
What a fellowship, what a joy divine 110
What a friend we have in Jesus ... 198
What armor must he wear ... 112
WHAT MUST I DO TO BE SAVED ... 86
What tow'rs are those that rise ... 64
WHAT WONDROUS LOVE ... 43
When bowed with affliction ... 15
WHEN HE CALLS HIS CHILDREN ... 148
When I walked with my Lord in tho. 161
When I was far away from God ... 52
When our hearts are sad and weary.. 102
When passed are tears and laughter.. 118
When storms around are sweeping ... 59
WHEN THE SHADOWS FLEE AWAY ... 55
WHEN WE ALL GET HOME OVER ... 26
When your heart is troubled ... 135
WHERE HE LEADS I'LL FOLLOW ... 104
WHERE THE LIVING WATERS FLOW... 160
WHY NOT BE SAVED ... 6
WHY STAND YE HERE IDLE ... 40
WILL YOU BE THERE ... 70
WILL YOU MEET US ... 167
WONDERFUL GOSPEL ... 69
WONDERFUL LOVE OF GOD ... 72
WORDS OF SPIRIT AND LIFE ... 120
Ye messengers of grace ... 106
Ye people of the Lord bowed with ... 21
YOUNG MEN AND MAIDENS ... 39
Youth is the seed time ... 149

INDEX OF SUBJECTS.

Activity, 4, 10, 12, 14, 17, 22, 29, 32, 40, 46, 56, 73, 94, 96, 98, 121, 188.
Atonement, 7, 11, 92, 182, 189, 204.
Bible, 58, 69, 93, 120.
Children's Day, 9, 17, 28, 95, 100, 177, 178.
Christ—
  Advent of, 173, 174, 175, 183.
  Life of, 2.
  Death of, 38, 57, 74, 92.
  Resurrection of, 176.
  Glory of, 27, 34, 168.
  Second Advent of, 21, 144.
  A Friend, 88, 147, 138.
  A Fountain, 23, 25, 80, 122, 160, 207.
  A King, 37, 89, 157, 158.
  A Refuge, 63, 102, 103, 110, 123, 155, 162, 166, 206.
  A Savior, 19, 22, 182, 189.
  A Shepherd, 104, 129, 199.
Christian Endeavor, 39, 41, 46, 125, 128, 130, 157, 169, 186.
Closing, 49, 137, 140.
Coming to Christ, 116, 165, 190, 191.
Confessing Christ, 36, 76, 163, 200, 204, 211.
Consecration, 5, 53, 76, 97, 141, 169, 187, 190.
Death, 15, 24, 38, 54, 64, 82, 133, 170, 209.
Dependence, 110, 135, 145, 162, 166, 187.
Epworth League, 39, 96, 128, 157, 169, 186.
Evening, 105, 152.
Faith, 7, 81, 84, 200.
Giving, 98, 143.
Grace, 30, 42, 101.
Harvest Home, 4, 10, 143, 149, 154.
Heaven, 24, 26, 31, 34, 44, 54, 55, 64, 70, 78, 79, 82, 117, 118, 133, 148, 164, 167, 170, 205.
Holy Spirit, 3, 8, 13, 16, 153.
Infant Class, 48, 53, 61, 69, 109, 113, 124, 135.
Invitation, 3, 6, 13, 14, 23, 25, 52, 65, 68, 70, 80, 108, 110, 114, 139, 142, 184, 185, 189, 193, 203, 210.
Jesus, 20, 27, 33, 38, 48, 88, 91, 107, 131, 138, 181.
Joy, 1, 10, 18, 66, 77, 111, 115, 134, 138, 160, 164, 195.
Judgment, 21, 50, 108.
Love, 2, 5, 11, 15, 19, 38, 43, 48, 49, 60, 67, 72, 83, 91, 109, 113, 186, 197.
Male Chorus, 59, 102.
Missionary, 99, 106, 146.
Obedience, 104, 126, 132, 161.
Opening, 19, 28, 35.
Praise, 9, 19, 20, 27, 28, 37, 39, 76, 87, 89, 100, 131, 168, 180.
Prayer, 35, 59, 62, 179, 194, 196, 198.
Providence, 15, 30, 61.
Pilgrimage, 71, 127, 136, 144, 192.
Repentance, 50, 86.
Rest, 60, 166.
Sabbath Day, 90, 172.
Salvation, 1, 19, 47, 68, 85, 92, 141, 156, 160, 184, 208.
Temperance, 124.
Thanksgiving, 154.
Trust, 51, 118, 119, 129, 161, 171, 185.
Warfare, 45, 71, 75, 94, 112, 157, 158, 159, 163, 169.

Lightning Source UK Ltd.
Milton Keynes UK
UKHW021854121118
332198UK00006B/267/P

9 780483 712331